Berlitz

English

phrase book & dictionary

D1498591

L.C.C.

CHARLES DICKENS
1812-1870
Novelist
Lived Here

H46 552 532 8

Contacting the Editors
Every effort has been made to provide accurate information in this publication, but changes are inevitable. The publisher cannot be responsible for any resulting loss, inconvenience or injury. We would appreciate it if readers would call our attention to any errors or outdated information. We also welcome your suggestions; if you come across a relevant expression not in our phrase book, please contact us at: **comments@berlitzpublishing.com**

Eleventh Printing: September 2012
Printed in China

Publishing Director: Mina Patria
Commissioning Editor: Kate Drynan
Editorial Assistant: Sophie Cooper
Phonetic transcription: Sinda López
Cover Design: Beverley Speight
Interior Design: Beverley Speight
Production Manager: Raj Trivedi
Picture Researcher: Beverley Speight
Cover Photo: All photos Ming Tang Evans/APA except iStock currency photo and NY cab; old building Tony Halliday/APA; red post box Corrie Wingate/APA

Interior Photos: Ming Tang Evans/APA 1, 19, 20, 24, 28, 49, 50, 53, 92, 102, 105, 130, 151; NowitzTeam/APA 14, 26, 30, 33, 56, 85, 98, 97, 109, 111, 116, 119, 134; istockphoto 23, 36, 42, 44, 45, 64, 66, 69, 70, 79, 81, 88, 89, 90, 91, 110, 120, 132, 141, 142, 145, 147, 148, 150, 166, 167 Mina Patria/APA; 34, 41, 122 Kevin Cummins/APA 37; Britta Jaschiniski/APA 39, 74, 76, 87, 133; Bev Speight/APA 47; William Shaw/APA 54, 137; Frank Noon/APA 59; Corrie Wingate/APA 60, 62, 95, 123, 125, 126; Sylvaine Pontau/APA 73, 83; Tim Thompson/APA 139; Greg Gladman/APA 113, 115, 138; Tony Halliday/APA 129; Lucy Johnston/APA 170

Contents

Food & Drink

People

Leisure Time

Special Requirements

In an Emergency

Dictionary

Pronunciation

This section is designed to make you familiar with the sounds of English using our simplified phonetic transcription. You'll find the pronunciation of the English letters and sounds explained below, together with their 'imitated' equivalents. This system is based on sounds of familiar English words and is used throughout the phrase book.

Note also the special rules below.

Underlined letters indicate that syllable should be stressed.

The g of the '-ing' ending is almost silent.

Consonants

Letter	Approximate Pronunciation	Example	Symbol	Pronunciation
b	like the b in	**bed**	b	*bEd*
c	1. before e and i like the s in	**scent**	s	*scEnt*
	2. otherwise like the k in kit	**cat**	k	*kat*
	3. ch like in	**chat**	tch	*tchat*
	or	**much**		*mUtch*
d	1. like the d in	**do**	d	*du*
f	1. at the start or in the middle of a word like the f in	**for**	f	*for*
		of		
	2. at the end of a word like the v in	**very**	v	*Ov*
g	1. like the g in	**get**	q	*gɛt*
	2. like the g in	**gentle**	dj	*djen•til*
h	1. lIke the h in	**hello**	h	*he•lou*
	2. silent like in	**honest**	-	*On•ist*

Letter	Approximate Pronunciation	Example	Symbol	Pronunciation
j	like the j in	**jeans**	j	*jeens*
k	1. like the k in	**key**	k	*kee*
	2. silent like in	**know**	n	*nou*
l	like the l in	**leg**	l	*lEg*
m	like the m in	**man**	m	*man*
n	like the n in	**no**	n	*nou*
p	like the p in	**pen**	p	*pEn*
q	usually qu like in	**queen**	ku	*kueen*
r	1. at the start of a word like the r in	**red**	r	*rEd*
	2. at the end of a syllable, almost silent like in	**park**	-	*pArk*
s	1. like the s in	**see**	s	*see*
	2. sh like the sh in	**shut**	sh	*shUt*
t	1. like the t in	**ten**	t	*tEn*
	2. th like the th in	**the**	dh	*dhe*
	3. th like the th in (with the tip of the tongue placed between the front teeth)	**thank**	tz	*tzank*
v	like the v in	**very**	v	*vE•ree*
w	1. like the w in (lips move forward into a whistle position, then pull back into a smile position)	**well**	w	*wEl*
	2. sometimes silent	**who**	h	*hu*

Letter	Approximate Pronunciation	Example	Symbol	Pronunciation
x	like the x in	**six**	ks	*siks*
y	1. like the y in	**yes**	y	*yEs*
	2. at the end of a word like the y in	**my**	ai	*mai*
	3. at the end of a word that has 2 or more syllables like the y in	**daily**	ee	<u>*dei*</u>•*lee*
z	1. like the z in	**zoo**	zz	*zzu*
	2. at the end of a word like the th in	**with**	z	*wiz*

Vowels

In English, vowels can have a short or long pronunciation. With A, E, O and U, the main short sound is represented by the normal lower case letter and the long pronunciation by a capital letter, for example: dhe End. This rule hasn't been implemented for the 'I' because of confusion when it stands alone as a subject pronoun. The long 'I' sound is transcribed as 'ai'.

Letter	Approximate Pronunciation	Example	Symbol	Pronunciation
a	1. like the a in	**and**	**a** (short; strong)	*and*
	2. like the a in	**alive**	**ah** (short; weak)	*ahlaiv*
	3. like the a in	**father**	**A** (long)	*f<u>A</u>.dhe*
	4. like the a in	**name**	ei	*neim*
	5. like the a in	**care**	**E**	*kEr*

Letter	Approximate Pronunciation	Example	Symbol	Pronunciation
e	1. like the e in	**the**	e (short)	*dhe*
	2. like the e in	**end**	e (long)	*End*
	3. like the e in	**employ**	i	*im-ploi*
i	1. like the i in	**in**	i	*in*
	2. like the i in	**ice**	ai	*aise*
o	1. like the o in	**for**	o	*for*
	2. like the o in	**dollar**	O	*dO-lah*
	3. like the o in	**other**	U	*U-dhe*
	4. like the o in	**over**	ou	*ou-vah*
	5. like the o in	**do**	u	*du*
	6. like the o In	**one**	w	*wUn*
u	1. like the u in	**rule**	u	*rul*
	2. like the u in	**uncle**	U	*Un-kel*
	3. like the u in	**use**	yu	*yus*

Other common vowel combinations

Letter	Approximate Pronunciation	Example	Symbol	Pronunciation
ai	like the ai in	**paid**	e (long)	*peid*
au	like the au in	**autumn**	oh	*oh.tum*
aw	like the aw in	**law**	oh	*loh*
ay	like the a in	**say**	ei	*sei*
ea	1. like the ea in	**eat**	ee	*eet*
	2. like the ea in	**earn**	U	*Urn*
ee	like the ee in	**see**	ee	*see*
ei	like the ei in	**eight**	ei	*eit*
oo	1.like the oo in	**book**	uh	*buhk*
	2. like the oo in	**food**	u	*fud*
	3. like the oo in	**door**	oh	*dohr*

Letter	Approximate Pronunciation	Example	Symbol	Pronunciation
ou	like the ou in	**sound**	au	*saund*
ow	1. like the ow in	**town**	au	*taun*
	2. like the ow in	**slow**	ou	*slou*
oy	like the oy in	**boy**	oi	*boi*
ough	1. like the ough in	**cough**	Off	*kOff*
	2. like the ough in	**bought**	ohrt	*bohrt*
	3. like the ough in	**tough**	u	*tuff*
		bough		*bow*
		though		*thoh*
		through		*tzru*
uy	like the uy in	**buy**	ai	*bai*

How to use this Book

> This Essential traveler information can be heard on the audio CD.

ESSENTIAL

Where's...?   *wErs...?*
   the nearest ATM   *dhe neerEst ei-tee-Em*
   [cash machine]   *kash mah-sheen*
   the bank   *dhe bank*

> Symbols you may see are shown in YOU MAY SEE boxes.

YOU MAY SEE...

drinking water   *drink•in woh•ter*

no camping   *nou kamp•in*

> Phrases you may say are shown in You May Say boxes.

YOU MAY SAY...

I can't understand you,   *ai kant Un•der•stand yu, kan*
can you repeat that?   *yu ripeet dhat?*

Baby Essentials

Do you have...?   *du yu hav...?*
   a pacifier [dummy]   *ah pas•i•faiy•ah [dUmee]*
   a playpen   *ah pleipEn*
   a stroller [pushchair]   *ah strouler*
Can I breastfeed the
baby here?

> Sometimes different words are used in British and American English. When this is the case, you will be given the British word in brackets.

U.S. and U.K. spelling is sometimes different for the same word.

A simplified phonetic transcription is given to help you with pronunciation. For more explanations, see page 7.

Hair & Beauty

I'd like...
aid laik...

an appointment for today/tomorrow
ahn ah·point·ment for tUdei/tU·mO·rou

some color [colour]/ highlights
seim kUlUr/hailaits

my hair styled/ blow dried
mai hEr staild/blou-draid

For Clothes & Accessories, see page 117.

Related phrases can be found by going to the page number indicated.

Sometimes you see two alternatives separated by a slash. Choose the one that's right for your situation.

When meeting someone for the first time, it is normal to shake hands in both the United Kingdom and in the United States. It is not the culture to kiss someone you do not know on the cheek. However, people will often smile and say hello to people even if they do not know them, especially in sm

Information boxes contain relevant country, culture and language tips.

Expressions you may hear can be heard on the audio CD.

YOU MAY HEAR...

Turn off your mobile phones, please.
tUrn Off yor moubile founs, plees.

Color-coded side bars identify each section of the book.

Survival

Arrival & Departure

ESSENTIAL

Your passport, please.	yor *pAs*•port, plees
What's the purpose of your visit?	wUts dhe *pUr*•pUs Ov yor *vi*•sit
I'm on vacation [holiday]/ business.	aim on vei•*kei*•shUn [hO•li•dei] / *bis*•nis
Where are you staying?	wEr Ar yu *stei*•yin
I'm going to...	aim *gouin* tu...
I'm staying at the...Hotel.	aim *stei*•yin at dhe...hou•*tEl*
How long are you staying?	hau lOng Ar yu *stei*•yin
Who are you here with?	hu Ar yu heer wiz

Border Control

I'm just passing through.	aim jUst *pAs*•ing tzru
I'd like to declare...	aid laik tu de•*klEr*...
I have nothing to declare.	ai hav *nU*•tzing tu de•*klEr*

When passing through border control, you may be taken aside to be searched. This may be your bag, or you may have a **body search** or **pat down** (as it is known in the U.S.). These searches are becoming more and more frequent and form part of a routine security check carried out in both U.S. and U.K. airports.

Money

ESSENTIAL

Where's...?	*wErs...*
the nearest ATM	*dhe neerEst ei·tee·Em*
[cashpoint]	*[kash·point]*
the bank	*dhe bank*
Where can I change money?	*wEr kan ai tcheindj mU·nee*
My card has been...	*mai kArd has been...*
blocked	*blOkd*
swallowed	*sWohl·laud*
Can I call my branch from here?	*kan ai kol mai brAnch frOm heer*
Where can I get a pre-paid credit card?	*wEr kan ai gEt ah pree·peid krE·dit kArd*

At the Bank

I'd like to change money/get a cash advance.	*aid laik tu tcheindj mU·nee/gEt ah kash ahd· vAns*

The currency in the U.S., Canada, Australia and New Zealand is in dollars and cents, but in Britain it is in pounds and pence. Pence is shortened to p (pronounced '**pee**'), so instead of saying **60 pence**, the British say **60p**. For items costing more than £1, it is usual just to say, for example, **one pound 25**, not **one pound 25p**.

What's the exchange rate/fee?	*wUts dhe Eks•tcheindj reit/fee*
I think there's a mistake.	*ai tzink dhErs ah mis•teik*
I lost my traveller's cheques.	*ai lOst mai tra•vel•ahs tchEks*
My card...	*mai kArd...*
was lost	*wUs lOst*
was stolen	*wUs stou•len*
doesn't work	*dUs•ent wUrk*

Most banks in Britain are open from 9.30 a.m. to 4.30 p.m. Monday-Friday, with Saturday morning banking common in shopping areas. In the U.S., banks open from 9.00 a.m. to 5.00 p.m. on weekdays, with some open late until 6.00 p.m., and on Saturdays. The majority of bank branches have **ATMs [cashpoints]** where international credit or **cashpoint [debit]** cards can be used to withdraw cash. Some high-street travel agents operate bureaux de change. Many privately run bureaux de change are open 24 hours, but generally, exchange rates can be low but commissions high. Pre-paid credit cards are a cost-effective way to travel with holiday money.

Getting Around

ESSENTIAL

How do I get to town?	*hau du ai gEt tu taun*
Where's...?	*wErs...*
the subway [underground] station	*dhe <u>sUb</u>•wei [<u>Un</u>•de•graund] <u>stei</u>•shUn*
Is it far from here?	*is it fA frOm heer*
Where do I buy a ticket?	*wEr du ai bai ah <u>ti</u>•kit*
A one-way [single]/ round trip [return] ticket to...	*ah wUn-<u>wei</u> [<u>sin</u>•gel]/raund-trip [ri•<u>tUrn</u>] <u>ti</u>•kit tu...*
How much?	*hau mUtch*
Which gate/line?	*witch geit/lain*
Which platform?	*witch <u>plat</u>•fohrm*
Where can I get a taxi?	*wEr kan ai gEt ah <u>taks</u>•ee*
Do I need to go to a taxi rank?	*du ai need tu go tu ah <u>taks</u>•ee rank*
Take me to this address.	*teik mee tu dhis ah•<u>drEss</u>*

Tickets

When's...to Paris?	*wEns... tu Paris*
the (first) bus	*dhe (ferst) bUs*
the (next) flight	*dhe (<u>nEkst</u>) flait*

the (last) train	*dhe (lAst) trein*
Where do I buy a ticket?	*wEr du ai bai ah ti·kit*
One /Two ticket(s) please.	*wUn/tu ti·kit(s), plees*
For today/ tomorrow.	*for tU·dei/tU·mO·rou*
A…ticket.	*ah ti·kit*
one-way	*wUn-wei*
return trip	*ri·tUrn trip*
first class	*ferst klAs*
business class	*bis·nis klAs*
economy class	*i·kOn·U·mee klAs*

A ticket to go and return is called a **round trip ticket** in the United States and a **return** ticket in the United Kingdom. A ticket that only goes and does not return is called a **one-way ticket** in the United States and a **single** ticket in the United Kindgom.

How much?	*hau mUtch*
Is there a discount for...?	*is dhEr ah dis•kount for...*
children	*tchil•drin*
students	*styu•dents*
senior citizens	*seen•yUr si•ti•zzens*
tourists	*tu•rists*
The express bus/ train, please.	*dhe Eks•pres bUs/trein, plees*
The local bus/ train, please.	*dhe lou•kel bUs/trein, plees*
I have an e-ticket.	*ai hav ahn ee-ti•kit*

YOU MAY HEAR...

What airline are you flying?	*wUt Er•lain Ar yu flai•in*
Domestic or international?	*dU•mEs•tik or in•ter•na•shUn•el*
What terminal?	*wUt ter•min•el*

The U.K.'s two major international airports are Heathrow, which is 15 miles (24 km) to the west of London, and Gatwick, which is 24 miles (40 km) south of the capital. An increasing number of international flights now arrive at the regional airports of Birmingham, Manchester, Liverpool, Glasgow, Prestwick and Cardiff, as well as London's other airports, Stansted and Luton. The small London City Airport, a few miles from London's financial heart, is used by small aircraft to fly to European capitals.

Most travelers arriving in the United States do so by air. The major U.S. cities with international airports are New York, Miami, Washington DC, Los Angeles, Atlanta and San Diego. From these cities, connecting flights can be made all over the U.S. to secondary cities and towns.

Can I buy…	*kan ai bai…*
a ticket on the bus/ train?	*ah ti·kit on dhe bUs/trein*
the ticket before boarding?	*dhe ti·kit bee·for bor·ding*
How long is this ticket valid?	*hau lOng is dhis ti·kit va·lid*
Can I return on the same ticket?	*kan ai ri·tUrn On dhe seim ti·kit*
I'd like to…my reservation.	*aid laik tu… mai rE·ser·vei·shUn*
cancel	*kan·sel*
change	*tcheindj*
confirm	*kOn·ferm*

YOU MAY HEAR...

Next!	*nEkst*
Your passport/ticket, please.	*yor pAs•port/ti•kit, plees*
Are you checking [in] any luggage?	*Ar yu tchEk•in [in] E•nee lU•gitch*
That's too large for a carry-on [piece of hand luggage].	*dhAts tu lArj for ah ka•ree-on [peezz Ov hand lU•gitch]*
Did you pack these bags yourself?	*did yu pak dhees bags yor•sElf*
Did anyone give you anything to carry?	*did E•nee•wUn giv yu E•nee•tzin tu ka•ree*
Take off your shoes/belt.	*Teik Off yor shus/bElt*
Now boarding...	*Nau bor•din...*

Plane

Airport Transfer

How much is a taxi to the airport?	*hau mUtch is ah taks•ee tu dhe Er•port*
To...Airport, please.	*Tu...Er•port, pleese*
My airline is...	*mai Er•lain is...*
My flight leaves at...	*mai flait leevs at...*
I'm in a rush.	*aim in ah rUsh*
Can you take an alternate route?	*kan yu teik ahn ol•ter•net rut*
Can you drive faster/ slower?	*kan yu draiv fAs•ter/slou•er*

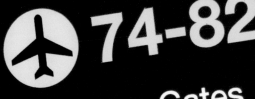

Checking In

Where's check-in?	*wErs tchEk-in*
My name is…	*mai neim is…*
I'm going to…	*aim gouin tu…*
I have…	*ai hav…*
one suitcase	*wUn sut•keis*
two suitcases	*tu sut•keises*
one piece	*wUn peezz*
How much luggage is allowed?	*hau mUtch lU•gitch is ah•laud*
Is that pounds or kilos?	*is dhat paunds or kee•lous*
Which terminal?	*witch ter•min•el*
Which gate?	*witch geit*
I'd like a window/ an aisle seat.	*aid laik ah win•dou/ahn ai•yUl seet*
When do we leave/ arrive?	*wEn du wee leev/ah•raiv*
Is the flight delayed?	*is dhe flait di•leid*
How late?	*hau leit*

Luggage

Where is/are…?	*wEr is/Ar…*
the luggage trolleys	*dhe <u>lU</u>•gitch <u>trO</u>•lees*
the luggage lockers	*dhe <u>lU</u>•gitch <u>lO</u>•kers*
the baggage claim	*dhe <u>ba</u>•gitch kleim*
My luggage has been lost/stolen.	*mai lU•gitch has been lOst/<u>stou</u>•len*
My suitcase is damaged.	*mai <u>sut</u>•keis is <u>da</u>•mitcht*

Finding your Way

Where is/are…?	*wEr is/Ar…*
the currency exchange	*dhe <u>kU</u>•ren•cee Eks•<u>tchein</u>•dj*
the car hire	*dhe kAr <u>hai</u>•yah*
the exit	*dhe <u>Eks</u>•it*
the taxis	*dhe <u>taks</u>•ees*
Is there…	*is dhEr…*
into town?	*<u>in</u>•tu taun*

In the United Kingdom, railways are run by 27 private regional operating companies. They are not known for punctuality, so if your arrival time is critical allow for possible delays. There are many money-saving deals, such as cheap-day returns, available. Generally tickets bought at least two weeks in advance are much cheaper than standard rates, but they sell out fast.

Amtrak is the major rail passenger carrier in the U.S. and its network links many cities. However, the United States are so huge that, for most people, the only logical way to get around is by flying.

a bus	*ah bUs*
a train	*ah trein*
a subway/the underground	*ah sUb•wei / dhe Un•de•graund*

Train

Where's the train station?	*wErs dhe trein stei•shUn*
How far is it?	*hau fAr is it*
Where is/are...?	*wEr is/Ar...*
the ticket office	*dhe ti•kit O•ffiss*
the information desk	*dhe in•for•mei•shUn desk*

YOU MAY HEAR...

Tickets, please.	*ti•kits, plees.*
You have to change at...	*yu hav tu tcheindj at...*
Next stop...	*nEkst stOp...*

In some U.S. and U.K. cities, you can purchase one **transportation [transport] card** and use it on both the bus and the **subway [underground].** The card can often be **refilled [topped up]** at vending machines, so you can use the same card over and over. Discount cards are often available for tourists and people over 65. Children under 4 or under a certain height regularly **ride [travel]** for free. Visit the webpage of the **transit [transport]** authority for the city you're visiting for more information.

the luggage lockers	*dhe _lU_•gitch _lO_•kers*
the platforms	*dhe _plat_•fohrms*
Can I have a schedule [timetable]?	*kan ai hav ah _shEd_•yul [_taim_•tei•bel]*
How long is the trip?	*hau lOng is dhe trip*
Is it a direct train?	*is dhEr ah _dai_•rEkt trein*
Do I have to change trains?	*du ai hav tu tcheindj treins*
Is the train on time?	*is dhe trein on taim*

Departures

Which track [platform] to…?	*witch trak [plat•fohrm] tu…*
Is this the track [platform]/train to…?	*is dhis dhe trak [plat•fohrm]/trein tu…*
Where is track [platform]…?	*wEr is trak [plat•fohrm]…*
Where do I change for…?	*wEr du ai tcheindj for…*

On Board

Can I sit here/open the window?	*kan ai sit heer/ou•pen dhe win•dou*
That's my seat.	*dhats mai seet*
Here's my reservation.	*heers mai rE•ser•vei•shUn*

Bus

Where's the bus station?	*wErs dhe bUs stei•shUn*
How far is it?	*hau fAr is it*

In the United States, public transport facilities vary widely and not all cities have a wide range of public transport options. The New York City **subway** system is the only subway system in the world that runs 24/7. The London Underground, or '**the Tube**', is Britain's most extensive public transport system.

There are also different pre-paid systems for public transport. In New York City you use a **MetroCard** for buses and subways. In London you buy an **Oyster Card** which works on buses and tubes and overland trains. In Sydney, you use **MyZone** tickets for ferries as well as trains and buses.

How do I get to…?	*hau du ai gEt tu…*
Is this the bus to…?	*is dhis dhe bUs tu…*
Can you tell me when to get off?	*kan yu tEl mee wEn tu gEt Off*
Do I have to change buses?	*du ai hav tu tcheindj <u>bUs</u>•is*
Stop here, please!	*stOp heer, plees*

Subway & Underground

Where's the subway/ underground station?	*wErs dhe <u>sUb</u>•wei /<u>Un</u>•de•graund <u>stei</u>•shUn*
A map, please.	*ah map, plees*
Which line for…?	*witch lain for…*
Which direction?	*witch dai•<u>rEk</u>•shUn…*
Do I have to transfer [change]?	*du ai hav tu <u>trAns</u>•fer [tcheindj]*
Is this the subway /underground to…?	*is dhis dhe <u>sUb</u>•wei / <u>Un</u>•de•graund tu…*
How many stops to…?	*hau <u>mE</u>•nee stOps tu…*
Where are we?	*wEr Ar wee*

Boat & Ferry

When is the ferry to…?	*wEn is dhe fe•ree tu…*
Can I take my car?	*kan ai teik mai kAr*
What time is the next sailing?	*wUt taim is dhe nEkst sei•lin*
Can I book a seat/cabin?	*kan ai buhk ah seet/ka•bin*
How long is the crossing?	*hau lOng is the krO•sin*

Taxi

Where can I get a taxi?	*wEr kan ai gEt ah taks•ee*
Can you send a taxi?	*kan yu sEnd ah taks•ee*
Do you have the number for a taxi?	*du yu hav dhe nUm•bah for ah taks•ee*
I'd like a taxi now/ for tomorrow at…	*aid laik ah taks•ee nau/for tU•mO•rou at…*
Pick me up at…	*pik mee Up at…*
I'm going to…	*aim gou•in tu…*
this address	*dhis ah•dress*
the airport	*dhe Er•port*
the train station	*dhe trein stei•shUn*
I'm late.	*aim leit*
Can you drive faster/ slower?	*kan yu draiv fAst•er/slou•er*
Stop/Wait here.	*stOp/Weit heer*
How much?	*hau mUtch*
You said it would cost…	*yu sEd it wuhd cost…*
Keep the change.	*keep dhe tcheindj*

YOU MAY HEAR...

Where to?	*wEr tu*
What's the address?	*wUts dhe ah•dress*
There's a nighttime/	*dhErs ah nait-taim/*
airport/baggage surcharge.	*Er•port/bag•ahDj*
	ser•tchArdj

As soon as you enter a taxi, or cab, you're charged a fee, and
with every set distance driven, the fare increases. You may also be
charged a higher rate during peak hours and at night.
There is a 'bill of rights' for taxi passengers in the U.S. Passengers
have the right to pay by credit card, to specify the route, to request
air conditioning or heating, to have a noise-free and smoke-free **ride**
[journey] and more. If your cab driver provides poor service, you also
have the right not to tip. Otherwise, a small tip is common.

Bicycle & Motorbike

I'd like to hire...	*aid laik tu <u>hai</u>-yah...*
a bicycle	*ah <u>bai</u>•si•kel*
a moped	*ah <u>mou</u>•pEd*
a motorcycle	*ah <u>mou</u>•ter•sai•kel*
How much per day /week?	*hau mUtch per dei/week*
Can I have a helmet/lock?	*kan ai hav ah <u>hEl</u>•met/ lOk*
I have a puncture/ flat tyre.	*ai hav ah <u>pUnk</u>•tcher/flat <u>tai</u>-yah*

Car Hire

Where's the car hire?	*wErs dhe kAr <u>hai</u>-yah*
I'd like...	*aid laik...*
a cheap/small car	*ah tcheep/smohl kAr*
an automatic/ a manual	*ahn oh•tou•<u>ma</u>•tik*
air conditioning	*Er kUn•<u>di</u>•shUn•in*
a car seat	*ah kAr seet*
How much...?	*hau mutch...*
per day/week	*per dei/week*
per kilometer	*per ki•<u>lO</u>•mi•ter*
for unlimited mileage	*for Un•<u>li</u>•mi•tid <u>mai</u>litch*
with insurance	*wiz in•<u>shuh</u>•rUns*
Are there any discounts?	*Ar dhEr <u>E</u>•nee <u>dis</u>•kounts*

YOU MAY HEAR...

Do you have an international driver's license?	*du yu hav ahn int•er•na•shUn•el drai•vers lai•sens*
Your passport, please.	*yor pAs•port, plees*
Do you want insurance?	*du yu wahnt in•shuhr•Uns*
I'll need a deposit.	*ai•yUl need ah di•pO•sit*
Initial/Sign here.	*i•ni•shUl/sain heer*

Fuel Station

Where's the fuel station?	*wErs dhe fyuel stei•shUn*
Fill it up.	*fil it Up*
...euros, please.	*...yu•rous, plees*
I'll pay in cash/by credit card.	*ai•yUl pei kash/bai krE•dit kArd*

Asking Directions

Is this the way to...?	*is dhis dhe wei tu...*
How far is it to...?	*hau fAr is it tu...*
Where's...?	*wErs...*
...Street	*...street*
this address	*dhis ah•dress*
the highway [motorway]	*dhe hai•wei [mou•ter•wei]*
Can you show me on the map?	*kan yu shou mee On dhe map*
I'm lost.	*aim lOst*

Parking

Can I park here?	*kan ai pArk heer*

YOU MAY HEAR...

straight ahead	*streit ah•hEd*
left	*lEft*
right	*rait*
around the corner	*ah•raund dhe kor•ner*
opposite	*O•pe•sit*
behind	*bee•haind*
next to	*nEkst tu*
after	*Af•ter*
north/south	*norz/sauz*
east/west	*eest/wEst*
at the traffic lights	*at dhe tra•fik laits*
at the intersection	*at dhe in•ter•sEk•shUn*

Where's...?	*wErs...*
the parking garage	*dhe pArk•in ga•ritch*
the parking lot	*dhe pArk•in lOt [kAr pArk]*
[car park]	
the parking meter	*dhe pArk•in meet•ah*
How much...?	*hau mutch...*

per hour	*per au-ah*
per day	*per dei*
for overnight	*for ou·ver·nait*

Breakdown & Repair

My car broke down/ *mai kAr brouk daun/wount stArt*
won't start.
Can you fix it (today)? *kan yu fiks it (tU·dei)*
When will it be ready? *wEn wil it bee rE·dee*
How much? *hau mUtch*

Accidents

There was an accident. *dhEr wUs ahn ak·si·dent*
Call an ambulance/ *kohl ahn am·byu·lens/dhe pe·lees*
the police.

Road congestion is a problem in most towns and city centres
in the U.K. and parking is often restricted. Never leave your car
parked on a double yellow or red line, or in a place marked for permit
holders only. These are offences for which you can be fined. Either use a
meter or a car park, signposted by a white P on a blue background.

Places to Stay

ESSENTIAL

Can you recommend a hotel? *kan yu rE•kU•mEnd ah hou•tEl*

I made a reservation. *ai meid ah rE•ser•vei•shUn*

Do you have a room…? *du yu hav ah rum*

   with a bathroom *wiz ah bAz•rum*

   with air conditioning *wiz Er kUn•di•shUn•in*

Smoking or non-smoking? *smoukin or nOn smoukin*

How much? *hau mUtch*

Is breakfast included? *is brekfAst in•kludid*

Is there anything cheaper? *is dhEr E•nee•tzing tcheep•er*

When's check-out? *wEns tchEk-aut*

Can I leave this in the safe? *kan ai leev dhis in dhe seif*

What time do you lock up? *wUt taim du yu lOk Up*

Can I leave my bags? *kan ai leev mai bags*

Can I have my check [bill]/ a receipt? *kan ai huv mai tchEk [bIl]/ah ri•seet*

I'll pay in cash/ by credit card. *ai•yUl pei in kash/bai krE•dit/kArd*

Bed & Breakfast

Somewhere to Stay

Can you recommend...?	*kan yu ri•kU•mEnd...*
a hotel	*ah hou•tEl*
a hostel	*ah hOs•tel*
a campsite	*ah kamp•sait*
a bed and breakfast (B&B)	*ah bEd and brEk•fUst (bee and bee)*

A variety of places to stay exist in the United Kingdom, from smart luxury hotels in stately homes and castles, to bed-and-breakfasts (B&B) in private family homes or country farmhouses. Not all hotels include breakfast in their rates and they may add a service charge of 10-15%. It is advisable to book in advance, particularly at Christmas, Easter, over bank holiday weekends and throughout the summer.

In the U.S., chain hotels and motels are reliable, convenient, and often reasonably priced. Resorts and large hotels are often located on spacious properties outside the downtown area. Boutique inns and small historic hotels, on the other hand, are often located in converted historic buildings in the downtown area and offer more B&B-like charm.

What is it near?	*wUt is it neer*
How do I get there?	*hau du ai gEt dhEr*

At the Hotel

I have a reservation.	*ai hav ah rE•ser•vei•shUn*
My name is…	*mai neim is…*
Do you have a room…?	*du yu hav ah rum…*
with a toilet/shower	*wiz ah toi•let/shau•er*
with air conditioning	*wiz Er kUn•di•shUn•in*
that's smoking /non-smoking	*dhats smouk•in/nOn-smouk•in*
For…	*for…*
tonight	*tU•nait*
two nights	*tu naits*
a week	*ah week*
Do you have…?	*du yu have…*
a computer	*ah kUm•pyu•ter*
an elevator [a lift]	*ahn E•le•vei•ter [ah lift]*

(wireless) internet service	*(wai•er•les) in•ter•nEt ser•vis*
room service	*rum ser•vis*
a pool	*ah pul*
a gym	*ah jim*
I need...	*ai need...*
an extra bed	*ahn Eks•trah bEd*
a cot	*ah kOt*
a crib	*ah krib*

Price

How much per night/week?	*hau mUtch per nait/week*
Does that include breakfast/tax?	*dus dhat in•klud brEk•fUst/taks*
Are there any discounts?	*Ar dhEr E•nee dis•kounts*

Preferences

Can I see the room?	*kan ai see dhe rum*
I'd like a... room.	*aid laik a... rum*
better	*bE•ter*
bigger	*bi•ger*

cheaper	*tcheep·er*
quieter	*kuai·e·ter*
I'll take it.	*ai·yUl teik it*
No, I won't take it.	*Nou, ai wount teik it*

Questions

Where is/are…?	*wEr is/Ar…*
the bar	*dhe bAr*
the bathrooms	*dhe bAz·rums*
the elevator [lift]	*dhe E·le·vei·ter [lift]*
I'd like…	*aid laik…*
a blanket	*ah blank·it*
an iron	*ahn ai·yUn*
the room	*dhe rum*
key/key card	*kee/kee KArd*
a pillow	*ah pi·lou*
soap	*soup*
toilet paper	*toi·let pei·per*
a towel	*ah tauw·el*
Do you have an adapter for this?	*du yu hav ahn ah·dap·ter for dhis*

How do you turn on the lights?	*hau du yu tUrn On dhe laits*
Can you wake me at…?	*kan yu weik mee at…*
Can I leave this in the safe?	*kan ai leev dhis in dhe seif*
Can I have my things from the safe?	*kan ai have mai tzins frOm dhe seif*
Is there mail /a message for me?	*is dhEr meil/ah <u>mE</u>•sitch for mee*
Do you have a laundry service?	*du yu hav ah <u>lohn</u>•dree <u>ser</u>•vis*

In the U.S., ask for the **restroom** or the **bathroom**.
In the U.K., you ask **Where's the toilet?** or more informally,
Where's the loo?
In Canada, it's common to ask for the **washroom**.

Problems

There's a problem.	*dhErs ah <u>prOb</u>•lem*
I lost my key/key card.	*ai lOst mai kee/kee kArd*
I've locked my key/card in the room.	*aiv lOkt mai kee/kee kArd in dhe rum*
There's no hot water/toilet paper.	*dhErs nou hOt <u>who</u>•ter/<u>toi</u>•let <u>pei</u>•per*
The room is dirty.	*dhe rum is <u>dert</u>•ee*
There are bugs in the room.	*dhEr Ar bUgs in dhe rum*

the air conditioning	*dhe er kUn•di•shUn•in*
the fan	*dhe fan*
the heat [heating]	*dhe heet [heet•in]*
the light	*dhe lait*
the TV	*dhe tee-vee*
the toilet	*dhe toi•let*
…doesn't work.	*…dUs•ent wUrk*
Can you fix…?	*kan yu fiks…*
I'd like another room.	*aid laik ahn•U•dhe rum*

Checking Out

When's check-out?	*wEns tchEk-aut*
Can I leave my bags here until…?	*kan ai leev mai bags heer Un•til…*
Can I have an itemized bill/	*kan ai hav ahn ai•tem•aised bil/ah ri•seet*
I think there's a mistake.	*ai tzink dhErs ah mis•teik*
I'll pay in cash/ by credit card.	*ai•yUl pei in kAsh/bai krE•dit kArd*

Renting

I reserved an apartment/a room.	*ai ri·served ahn ah·pArt·ment*
My name is...	*mai neim is...*
Can I have the keys?	*kan ai hav dhe kees*
Are there...?	*Ar dhEr...*
dishes	*dish·is*
pillows	*pi·lous*
sheets	*sheets*
towels	*tauw·els*
kitchen utensils	*kitch·in yu·tEn·sils*
When do I put out the bins /recycling?	*wEn du ai puht aut dhe bins/ri·sai·klin*
...is broken.	*...is brouken.*
How does...work?	*hau dUs... wUrk*
the air conditioner	*dhe Er kUn·di·shUn·er*
the dishwasher	*dhe dish·wah·sh·er*
the freezer	*dhe free·zah*
the heater	*dhe heet·ah*
the microwave	*dhe mai·krou·weiv*
the refrigerator	*dhe ri·frij·e·reit·er*

| the stove | *dhe stouv* |
| the washing machine | *dhe wahsh•in mah•sheen* |

Domestic Items

I need...	*ai need...*
an adapter	*ahn ah•dapt•er*
aluminum [aluminium] foil	*a•lu•mi•nUm [a•lu•mi•ny•um] foil*
a bottle opener	*ah bO•tel ou•pen•er*
a broom	*ah brum*
a can opener	*ah kan ou•pen•er*
cleaning supplies	*kleen•in sU•plais*
a corkscrew	*ah kork•skru*
detergent	*di•ter•jent*
dishwashing liquid	*dish•wah•shin li•kuid*
bin bags	*bin bags*
a lightbulb	*ah lait•bUlb*
matches	*match•is*
a mop	*ah mOp*
napkins	*nap•kins*
paper towels	*pei•per tauw•els*
plastic wrap [cling film]	*plas•tik rap [kling film]*
a plunger	*ah plUnj•er*
scissors	*si•sUrs*
a vacuum cleaner	*ah vak•yum kleen•er*

For In the Kitchen, see page 80.

For Oven Temperature, see page 169.

At the Hostel

Is there a bed available?	*is dhEr ah bEd ah•vei•le•bel*
I'd like…	*aid laik…*
a single/ double room	*ah sin•gel/dUb•el rum*
a blanket	*ah blank•it*
a pillow	*ah pi•lou*
sheets	*sheets*
a towel	*ah tauw•el*
Do you have lockers?	*du yu hav lOk•ers*
When do you lock up?	*wEn du yu lOk Up*
Do I need a membership card?	*du ai need ah mEm•ber•ship kArd*
Here's my international student card.	*heers mai in•ter•na•shUn•el styud•ent kArd*

150 mtr.

Going Camping

Can I camp here?	*kan ai kamp heer*
Where's the campsite?	*wErs dhe <u>kamp</u>•sait*
What is the charge per day/week?	*wUt is dhe tchArdj per dei/week*
Are there…?	*Ar dhEr…*
cooking facilities	*<u>kuhk</u>•in fah•<u>si</u>•li•tees*
electric outlets	*i•<u>lEk</u>•trik*
laundry facilities	*<u>lohn</u>•dree fah•<u>si</u>•li•tees*
showers	*shauw•ers*
tents for hire	*tEnts for <u>hai</u>-yah*
Where can I empty the chemical toilet?	*wEr kan ai <u>Em</u>•tee dhe <u>kE</u>•mik•el <u>toi</u>•let*

YOU MAY SEE…

drinking water	<u>drink</u>•in <u>woh</u>•ter	
no camping	*nou <u>kamp</u>•in*	
no fires/barbecues	*nou <u>fai</u>-yahs/<u>bAr</u>•be•kyus*	

Communications

ESSENTIAL

Where's an internet cafe?	*wErs ahn in•ter•nEt ka•fei*
Can I access the internet/check my e-mail?	*kan ai ak•ses dhe in•ter•nEt/tchEk mai ee-meil*
How much per half hour/hour?	*hau mUtch per hAlf au-ah/au-ah*
How do I connect/ log on?	*hau du ai kU•nEkt/lOg On*
A phone card, please.	*ah foun kArd, plees*
Can I have your phone number?	*kan ai hav yor nUm•bah*
Here's my number/ e-mail.	*heers mai nUm•bah/ee-meil*
Can I speak to...?	*kan ai speek tu...*
Can you repeat that?	*kan yu ripeet dhat*
I'll call back later.	*ai•yUl kol bak leit•er.*
Where's the post office?	*wErs dhe poust O•ffiss*
I'd like to send this to...	*aid laik tu sEnd dhis tu...*

Online

Where's an internet cafe?	*wErs ahn in•ter•nEt ka•fei*
Does it have	

wireless internet?	*dUs it hav <u>wai</u>-er•les in•ter•nEt*
What is the WiFi password?	*wUt is dhe <u>wai</u>•fai pAs•wUrd*
Is the WiFi free?	*is dhe <u>wai</u>•fai free*
Do you have bluetooth?	*du yu hav <u>blu</u>•tuz*
Can you show me how to turn on/off the computer?	*kan yu shou mee hau tu tUrn On/Off dhe kUm•<u>pyu</u>•ter*
Can I...?	*kan ai...*
access the internet	*<u>ak</u>•ses*
check my e-mail	*tchEk mai <u>ee</u>-meil*
print	*print*
plug in/charge my laptop/ iPhone/iPad/ BlackBerry?	*plUg in/tchArdj mai <u>lap</u>•tOp/<u>ai</u>•foun/<u>ai</u>•pad/<u>blak</u>•be•ree*
access Skype?	*<u>ak</u>•ses skaip*
How much per half hour/hour?	*hau mUtch per hAlf <u>au</u>-ah/<u>au</u>-ah*
How do I...?	*hau du ai...*

YOU MAY SEE...

close	*klous*
delete	*de·leet*
e-mail	*ee-meil*
exit	*Ek·sit*
help	*hElp*
instant messenger	*in·stant mE·sin·jer*
internet	*in·ter·nEt*
log in	*lOg in*
new (message)	*nyu*
on/off	*On/Off*
open	*ou·pen*
print	*print*
save	*seiv*
send	*sEnd*
username/password	*yu·ser·neim/pAs·wUrd*
wireless internet	*wai·er·les in·ter·nEt*

connect /disconnect	*kU·nEkt/dis·kU·nEkt*
log on/off	*lOg On/lOg Off*
type this symbol	*taip dhis sim·bel*
What's your e-mail?	*wUts yor ee-meil*
My e-mail is...	*mai ee-meil is...*
Do you have a scanner?	*du yu hav ah ska·ner*

Social Media

Are you on Facebook/Twitter?	*Ar yu On feis·buhk/tuit·er*

What's your user name?	*wUts yor <u>yu</u>•ser neim*
I'll add you as a friend.	*<u>ai</u>•yUl ad yu as ah frEnd.*
I'll follow you on Twitter.	*<u>ai</u>•yUl <u>fO</u>•lou yu On <u>Tui</u>•ter*
Are you following...?	*Ar yu <u>fO</u>•lou•in...*
I'll put the pictures on Facebook/Twitter.	*<u>ai</u>•yUl puht dhe <u>pik</u>•tchers On <u>feis</u>•buhk/<u>tuit</u>•er*
I'll tag you in the pictures.	*<u>ai</u>•yUl tag yu in dhe <u>pik</u>•tchers*

Phone

A phone card/ prepaid phone, please.	*ah foun kArd/<u>pree</u>•peid foun, plees*
How much?	*hau mUtch*
Where's the pay phone?	*wErs dhe pei foun*
What's the area country code for...?	*wUts dhe <u>e</u>•ree•ah <u>KUn</u>•tree koud for...*

What's the number for Information?	wUts dhe <u>nUm</u>·bah for in·for·<u>mei</u>·shUn
I'd like the number for...	aid laik dhe <u>nUm</u>·bah for...
I'd like to call collect [reverse the charges].	aid laik tu kohl kU·<u>lEkt</u> [ri·<u>vers</u> dhe <u>tchardj</u>·is]
My phone doesn't work here.	mai foun <u>dUs</u>·ent wUrk heer

To make a long-distance call from a payphone in the U.S., use either a pre-paid calling card, available in airports, post offices, and a few other outlets, or your credit card, chich you can use at any phone: dial 800-CALLATT, key in your credit card number, and wait to be connected.

In the U.K. it is usually cheaper to use public phones than hotel phones. Some public phones take coins only, others take phone cards and/or credit cards, and some take all three. Phone cards can be bought from post offices and newsagents in varying amounts between £1 and £20.

People often say '**oh**' when they mean '**zero**', especially when giving phone numbers and post codes, e.g. 'My phone number is **three-seven-oh-one-oh-four-five**.'

What network are you on?	wUt <u>nEt</u>•wUrk Ar yu On
Is it 3G?	is it tzree jee
I have run out of credit/minutes.	ai hav rUn aut Ov <u>krEd</u>•it/<u>min</u>•its
Can I buy some credit?	kan ai bai sUm <u>krEd</u>•it
Do you have a phone charger?	du yu hav ah foun tchArdje

YOU MAY HEAR...

Who's calling?	hus <u>kohl</u>•in
Hold on.	hould On
I'll put you through to him/her.	<u>ai</u>•yUl puht yu tzru tu him/her
He's/She's not here/on another line.	hee/shee is nOt heer/On ahn•<u>U</u>•dhe lain
Would you like to leave a message?	wUd yu laik tu leev ah <u>mE</u>•sitch
Call back later/in ten minutes.	kohl bak <u>leit</u>•er/in tEn min•its
Can he/she call you back?	kan hee/shee kohl yu bak
What's your number?	wUts yor <u>nUm</u>•bah

To call abroad from the UK, dial 00 + country code + area code + phone number. To call from the U.S., dial 011 + country code + area code + phone number. If you are phoning the Caribean or Canada from the U.S, you do not need to dial 011 first, just dial 1 + area code + phone number.

In an emergency, dial **999 in the U.K.** and **911 in the U.S.** to call the police, fire brigade or ambulance.

Can I have your number?	*kan ai hav yor _nUm_•bah*
Here's my number.	*heers mai _nUm_•bah*
Please call/text me.	*Plees kohl/tEkst mee*
I'll call/text you.	*_ai_•yUl kohl/tEkst yu*

Telephone Etiquette

Hello. This is…	*he_lou_• dhis is…*
Can I speak to…?	*kan ai speek tu…*
Extension…	*Eks•_ten_•shUn…*
Speak louder/more slowly, please.	*speek _laud_•er/mor _slou_•lee, plees*
Can you repeat that?	*kan yu ri•_peet_ dhat*
I'll call back later.	*_ai_•yUl kohl bak leit•er*
Bye.	*Bai*

Fax

Can I send/receive a fax here?	*kan ai sEnd/ri•_seev_ ah faks heer*
What's the fax number?	*wUts dhe faks _nUm_•bah*
Please fax this to…	*Plees faks dhis tu…*

Post

Where's the post office/mailbox ?	*wErs dhe poust O•ffiss/meil•bOks*
A stamp for this postcard/letter to…	*ah stamp for dhis poust•kArd/lE•ter tu…*
How much?	*hau mUtch*
Send this package by airmail/express.	*SEnd dhis pak•itch bai Er•meil/Eks•pres*
A receipt, please.	*ah ri•seet, plees*

The postal code or zip code in the United States is written at the end of the address and is made up of numbers, e.g. 10013.
In the United Kingdom, a postcode is made up of letters and a numbers, e.g. W1H 2BQ.
It is important to include this code on correspondance in both the U.S. and the U.K.
Post offices in the U.K. are open from 9:00 a.m to 5:30 p.m Monday to Friday, and 9.00 a.m to 12:30 p.m on Saturday. Stamps are sold at post offices, selected shops and newsagents, some supermarkets and from machines outside larger post offices. In the U.S. the post office opening hours are 8:00 a.m to 4:00 or 5:30 p.m.

Food & Drink

Eating Out

ESSENTIAL

Can you recommend a good restaurant/ an inexpensive bar? *kan yu rE•kU•mEnd ah guhd res•ter•ahnt/ahn in•Eks• pEn•siv bAr*

Is there a traditional restaurant nearby? *is dhEr ah tra•di•shUn•el res•ter•ahnt neerbai*

A table for..., please. *ah teibel for..., plees*

I'm waiting for someone. *aim weitin for sUmwUn*

Where are the toilets? *wEr Ar dhe toilets*

We're ready (to order). *weer rEdee (tu order)*

What do you recommend? *wUt du yu rE•kU•mEnd*

I'd like... *aid laik...*

Can I have extra [some more]... *kan ai hav Ekstrah [sUm mor]...*

It's to go [take away]. *its tu gou [teik ahwei].*

The check [bill], please. *dhe tchEk [bil], plees*

Is service included? *is servis in•klud•id*

Can I pay by credit card/have a receipt? *kan ai pei bai krEdit kArd/hav ah riseet*

Where to Eat

Can you recommend...?	*kan yu rE•kU•<u>mEnd</u>. . .*
a restaurant	*ah <u>res</u>•ter•ahnt*
a bar	*ah bAr*
a cafe	*ah <u>ka</u>fei*
a fast food place	*ah fAst fud pleis*
a cheap restaurant	*ah tcheep <u>res</u>•ter•ahnt*
an expensive restaurant	*ahn Eks•<u>pEn</u>•siv <u>res</u>•ter•ahnt*
a restaurant with a good view	*ah <u>res</u>•ter•ahnt wiz ah guhd vyu*
an authentic/ a non-touristy restaurant	*ahn o•<u>zEn</u>•tik/ah nOn <u>turis</u>•tee <u>res</u>•ter•ahnt*

Reservations & Preferences

I'd like to reserve a table...	*aid laik tu ri<u>serv</u> ah <u>teibel</u>. . .*

A table for two, please.	*ah teibel for tu, plees*
I have a reservation.	*ai hav ah rE•ser•vei•shUn*
Can we sit…?	*kan wee sit…*
here/there	*heer/dhEr*
outside	*autsaid*
in a non-smoking area	*in ah nOn smoukin E•ree•a*
by the window	*bai dhe windou*
in the shade	*in dhe sheid*
in the sun	*in dhe sUn*
Where are the toilets?	*wEr Ar dhe toilets*

How to Order

Excuse me, sir/ma'am?	*Eks•kyuse mee, sir/mAm*
We're ready (to order).	*weer rEdee (tu order)*
The wine list, please.	*dhe wain list, plees*

YOU MAY SAY…

We're ready to order.	*weer rEdee tu order*
A few more minutes please...	*ah fyu mor m•i•nUts plees...*
What are you having?	*wUt Ar yu havin*
Can you recommend something?	*kan yu rE•kU•mEnd dhe sUmtzing...*
I'm allergic to...	*aim ah•ler•jik tu...*
Do you have anything without...	*du yu hav E•nee•tzin wizaut...*

YOU MAY SEE...

cover charge	*kUver tchArdj*
fixed price	*fiksd prais*
menu (of the day)	*mEnyu (Ov dhe dei)*
service (not) included	*servis (nOt) in•klud•id*
specials	*speshUls*

I'd like...	*aid laik...*
a bottle of...	*ah bOtel Ov...*
a carafe of...	*ah kahraf Ov...*
a glass of...	*ah glAs Ov...*
The menu, please.	*dhe mEnyu, plees*
Do you have...?	*du yu hav...*
a menu in English	*ah mEnyu in inglish*
a fixed price menu	*ah fiksd prais mEnyu*
a children's menu	*ah tchildrins mEnyu*
What do you recommend?	*wUt du yu rE•kU•mEnd*
What's this?	*wUts dhis*
What's in it?	*wUts in it*

Is it spicy?	is it _spaisee_
Without…, please.	wiz_aut_…, plees
It's to go [take away].	its tu gou [teik ahwei]
I'd like…	aid laik…
More…, please.	mor…, plees.
With/Without…	wiz/wiz_aut_…
I can't eat…	ai kAnt eet…
rare	rEr
medium	_mee_dyum
well done	wEl dUn

Cooking Methods

baked beikt	cooked in a hot oven, usually cakes and pies but potatoes can also be baked
boiled boild	cooked on a stove in a pan of boiling water
braised breizd	this method is used for cooking meat; it is first fried on a very high heat for a short time and then placed in a pot under a lid and cooked on a low heat for 2-3 hours
breaded brEdid	covered in bread crumbs, usually fish or meat
creamed kreemd	cooked in milk or cream
diced daisd	cut into small cubes
filleted fi•lit•id	a piece of meat or fish with bones removed
fried fraid	cooked in oil in a frying pan on high or medium heat
grilled grild	cooked on or under an open wire grid (grill) placed over very hot surface or coals
poached poutcht	cooked by very slow boiling in a small amount of water, milk, stock or wine
roasted roustid	meat or vegetables cooked with dry heat over a fire or in the oven
sautéed souteid	cooked quickly over high heat in a small amount of oil or fat in a shallow pan
smoked smoukt	cooked with the help of smoke from burning wood

steamed *steemd*	cooked with the help of steam produced by boiling water
stewed *styud*	cooked very slowly over a low heat for a long time in a small amount of liquid
stuffed *stUft*	filled with a mix of ingredients, e.g. stuffed peppers can be filled with rice, mushrooms or vegetables

Dietary Requirements

I'm...	*aim...*
diabetic	*dai·ah·be·tik*
lactose intolerant	*laktous in·tOl·er·ent*
vegetarian	*vej·e·tEr·ee·an*
vegan	*veegUn*
I'm allergic to...	*aim ah·ler·jik tu*
I can't eat...	*ai kAnt eet...*
dairy products	*dEree prOdUkts*
gluten	*gluten*
nuts	*nUts*
pork	*pork*
shellfish	*shElfish*
spicy foods	*spaisee fuds*
wheat	*weet*
Is it halal/kosher?	*is it hahlal/koushah*

Do you have...?	du yu hav...
skimmed milk	skimd milk
whole milk	houl milk
soya milk	soiyah milk

Dining with Children

Do you have children's portions?	du yu hav tchildrins porshUns
A highchair/child's seat, please.	ah hai tchEr/tchailds seet, plees
Where can I feed/ change the baby?	wEr kan ai feed/tcheindj dhe beibee
Can you warm this?	kan yu wohrm dhis

For Traveling with Children, see page 137.

How to Complain

When will our food be ready?	wEn wil our fud bee rEdee
We can't wait any longer.	Wee kAnt weit Enee lOnger
We're leaving.	Weer leevin
I didn't order this.	ai dident order dhis
I ordered...	ai orderd...
I can't eat this.	ai kAnt eet dhis
This is too...	dhis is tu...
cold/hot	kould/hOt
salty/spicy	sohltee/spaisee
tough/bland	tIlf/bland
This isn't clean/ fresh.	dhis isUnt kleen/frEsh

Paying

The check [bill], please.	*dhe tchEk [bil], plees*
Separate checks [bills], please.	*sEpraht tchEks [bils], plees*
It's all together.	*its ohl tU•gE•dhe*
Is service included?	*is servis in•klud•id*
What's this amount for?	*wUts dhis amaunt for*
I didn't have that. I had…	*ai dident hav dhat. ai had…*
Can I have a receipt/ an itemized check [bill]?	*kan ai hav ah riseet/ahn ai•te•mai•sed tchEk [bil]*
That was delicious!	*dhat wUs de•li•shUs*
I've already paid.	*aiv ohl•rE•dee peid*

In the United Kingdom and in the United States, it is customary to leave a tip for the server, generally 15% of the total bill in the U.S. and 10% in the U.K. Increasingly, this service charge is included in the bill in the U.K. (and sometimes in the U.S. marked as '**gratuity**' [tip]) so it is worth checking before leaving a tip.

Meals & Cooking

Breakfast is often a very big meal, with cereal, eggs, sausage, bread, toast, jam, coffee, tea and juice. At noon, some people often have just a sandwich, but a lot of families have a big meal, especially on weekends. The evening meal is called **dinner** (U.S.) or **supper** (U.K.). On Sundays in the United States, a single meal called **brunch** often replaces breakfast and lunch. Traditionally, English **tea** is a meal of small sandwiches, scones (small cakes that are eaten with butter, jam and cream) and pastries, all served with a few cups of tea, of course.

Breakfast

American Breakfast

bacon [rashers]
beikUn [rA·shurs]
strips of cured ham

breakfast sausage
brEk·fahst sOsitch
ground meat sausage, usually pork or beef

eggs Benedict
Egz be·ne·dikt
egg and ham on toasted bread, served with creamy sauce

eggs over easy
Egz ou·vahr ee·zi
fried eggs with a runny yolk

French toast
FrEntch toust
bread soaked in egg and lightly fried, often served with syrup

grits *grits*
coarse corn porridge

home fries
houm fraiz
fried chunks of potato

maple syrup
meipl sirUp
sweet golden syrup from maple trees

pancake
pankeik
flat, fluffy round cake, usually eaten with butter and syrup

English Breakfast

bacon butty
bei•kUn bU•ti
'Butty' is another word for 'Sandwich', often served with tomato ketchup and sometimes egg

black pudding
blak puh•ding
a black sausage made from pork fat, pig's blood and oatmeal. Served sliced with cooked breakfast

continental breakfast
kon•tee•nen•tal brEk•fahst
usually includes a croissant and/or another French pastry, breads and jams, and a glass of orange juice

Full English breakfast
fuhl in•glish brEk•fahst
includes bacon, eggs, sausage, tomatoes, mushrooms, baked beans, toast and even a cup of tea. Also known as a 'fry-up'

porridge
pO•ridj
oats boiled in milk or water to produce a thick and soft dish, eaten hot

Scottish oatcakes
skO•tish out•keiks
a thin savoury biscuit made from oats

white pudding
wait puh•ding
a white sausage that contains pork fat and oatmeal Popular in Ireland and Scotland

American food portions are typically larger than in the U.K.,
so **appetizers [starters]** are not always necessary. Sweet
dishes such as pancakes and sugared cereals are more common for
breakfast in the U.S., but savory options are also available.
Cuisine can vary by region, for instance New England often has more
seafood and the Southwest has more spicy Mexican-influenced food.

Breads & Cakes

bagel *bei•gel*	a dense circular roll, often served with cream cheese and other toppings
bloomer *bluh•mah*	an oval bread with crusty top
bread rolls *brEd rolz*	small, round breads used as a side dish or for sandwiches, can be white or brown
corn bread *korn brEd*	sweet bread made from corn
crumpet *krUm•pit*	a small, round savoury cake with little holes on the top. Made from flour and yeast. Eaten hot with butter
Eccles cake *Ekls keik*	a small, round pastry filled with dried fruit
flapjack *flap•djak*	a sweet and chewy biscuit made from oats, butter, sugar and syrup. Usually baked and sold in flat, rectangular shapes
hot cross bun *hOt crOs bUn*	a small and sweet round cake with raisins and marked with a cross on the top, eaten at Easter
Madeira cake *mah•dEr•ah keik*	a rich sponge cake flavoured with lemon

mince pie
Mins pai

A small sweet pastry filled with dried fruit and spices such as cinnamon and nutmeg. Popular at Christmas

rock cake
rOk keik

A small cake with a rough 'rock-like' surface that is made with dried fruit and spices such as nutmeg

rye *rai*

Dark bread often containing seeds

scone
skounz

a small round cake made from flour and butter and can include raisins. Part of the English Cream Tea when served with strawberry jam and cream

Scotch pancake
skOtch pan·keik

Also known as 'dropped scones' these are a small pancake usually served with jam, cream or butter

shortbread
shoht·brEd

a rich crumbly biscuit made from flour, butter and sugar. Originated in Scotland

sliced pan
slaist pan

Bread produced in a large factory, pre-sliced and packaged for ease of use. Used for toast and sandwiches

soda bread
sou·dah brEd

a type of bread where baking soda is used instead of yeast. Raisins and nuts may be added

sourdough
sauah·dou

Slightly sour, tangy bread

wholegrain
houl·grein

brown bread with oats or seeds

wholemeal
houl·meel

a type of brown bread, may contain oats, bran or other whole grains

Appetizers

bruschetta
bruh•shE•tah
toasted bread topped with chopped tomato

cheese balls
tchees bawls
soft cheese mixed with herbs, served with crackers

buffalo wings
bUf•ah•lou wings
chicken wings coated in a spicy, tangy sauce

caesar salad
see•zah salUd
lettuce, cheese and croutons with egg-based dressing

chicken fingers
tchiken fin•gahz
fried chicken strips coated in breadcrumbs

chicken satay
tchiken sA•tei
chicken skewers in peanut sauce

chips *tchips*
fried potato strips [U.K.].

Cornish pasty
koh•nish pa•sti
a baked pastry filled with a mixture of meat and vegetables

crab cake *krab keik*
fried crab meat, bread crumbs and seasoning

crisps [potato chips]
krisps [pU•teit•ou tchips]
deep fried thin slices of potato, available in various flavors [flavours]

deviled egg
de•vild Eg
hard-boiled egg filled with cooked yolk mixed with mayonnaise

egg roll *Eg•roul*
fried spring rolls

knish *knish*
savory dumpling with meat and potato filling

mozzarella sticks
mO•tsah•rE•lah sticks
fried cheese coated in breadcrumbs

nachos *natchous*
corn chips served with peppers, melted cheese, and salsa

pigs in a blanket
Pigz in a blan•kit
a sausage wrapped in savory pastry [U.S.] or wrapped in bacon [U.K.]

pot-stickers
pOt sti•kahz
Meat dumpling

A very traditional and popular take-away food in Britain is **fish and chips**. The fish, usually cod, haddock or plaice, is deep fried in batter and served with chips and usually covered in salt and vinegar. In the U.S., a **burger and fries** would be a more common option than **fish and chips**.

pork scratching *pohk skra•tching*	fried pork skin, served cold. Also known as pork crackling
potato chips [crisps] *pU•tei•tou tchips [krisps]*	fried thin, crunchy slices of potato
sausage roll *soh•sidj rOl*	sausage meat baked in puff (light/flaky) pastry. Can be eaten hot or cold
Scotch egg *skOtch Eg*	a hard-boiled egg in a layer of sausage meat, covered with breadcrumbs. Served cold
Welsh Rarebit *WElsh rErbit*	cheese melted over toast seasonings (beer, red pepper or mustard)

Soup

chicken noodle *tchiken nudel*	chicken, noodles, and vegetables in broth Matzo ball broth with dumplings
clam chowder *klam tchau•dah*	a creamy soup with clams
cock-a-leekie *kOk•ah•lee•ki*	a Scottish soup made from boiled chicken and leek
French onion soup *FrEntch UnyUn sup*	onions in beef broth topped with melted cheese
lobster bisque *lObster bisk*	creamy soup with rich lobster flavor [flavour]

matzo ball *ma•tsou bohl*	broth with dumplings
mock turtle soup *mOk tUrtl sup*	a soup designed to taste like turtle soup without using turtles! Made with a calf's head or foot
mulligatawny *mU•li•gah•toh•ni*	a spicy, curry-flavoured Anglo-Indian soup. Usually contains meat and can be thickened with rice
oxtail soup *Oks•teil sup*	a thick, rich soup made from the tails of an ox
pea and mint soup *pee and mint sup*	a summer soup made with fresh garden peas and mint, served hot or cold with cream or cheese

Fish & Seafood

calamari *kah•lah•mA•ri*	fried squid
cockles *kOklz*	small salt-water clams sold in British seaside towns. They are usually freshly boiled with vinegar and pepper as seasoning
crayfish *krei•fish*	small shellfish, common in Southern U.S.
fish and chips *fish and tchips*	fillets of fish that are covered in batter (a mixture of eggs, milk and flour) and then fried and served with chips. The fish used is usually cod, haddock or plaice

fishcakes
fish•keiks

a small, round and flat mixture of fish and potato covered in breadcrumbs and cooked in oil

Fisherman's Pie
fi•shah•manz pai

a traditional pie containing cooked white fish and often prawns in a milk or béchamel sauce with a covering of mashed potato and cheese that is then baked together to serve hot

jellied eels
dje•lid eelz

chopped eels that are then boiled in water and vinegar to produce a jelly that can be eaten hot or cold. Very popular in Victorian London alongside Pie and Mash

lobster *lObster*

large red shellfish

potted shrimps
pO•tid shrimps

brown shrimp and butter with spices added for flavour. Traditionally eaten on bread

salmon *samUn*

pink fish that can be grilled, smoked or served raw

shrimp [prawn]
shrimp [prohn

small shellfish

Meat & Poultry

bacon [rashers]
bei•kUn [rA•shurs]

strips of cured ham

beef *beef*

red meat from the cow. Many different cuts are available

Breakfast is usually eaten before work or school, between 7:00 and 9:00 a.m.

Brunch is most commonly eaten on the weekends between 10:00 a.m and 2:00 p.m.

Lunch is often between 12:00 and 2:00 p.m and many people just eat a sandwich on-the-go.

Dinner is the most popular time to eat out and is typically had between 6:00 and 8:00 p.m. in the U.S. and between 7:00 to 9:00 p.m in the U.K.

chicken _tchiken_	neutral white tasting bird. Very versatile poultry and can be used in many dishes
duck _dUk_	rich, fatty bird with brown meat
ham _hAm_	pink, slightly salty meat, popular in sandwiches
lamb _lAm_	rich flavorsome red meat often flavored with mint and rosemary. Roast lamb is traditionally eaten on Easter Sunday in the U.K.
liver _liver_	rich dark red/brown organ
pheasant _fesUnt_	strong tasting game with brown meat
pork _pork_	white meat from the pig, usually roasted or as a chop
quail _kueil_	delicate, small bird
rabbit _rabit_	strong, white meat, popular in France and in stews
sausage _sOsitch_	minced pork rolled into cylinder shape. Popular for breakfast or in hot dogs
steak _steik_	expensive cut of beef, usually pan fried or grilled
turkey _tUrkee_	large bird with white meat, traditionally eaten at Christmas or Thanksgiving
veal _veel_	white, baby calf meat

venison _vEn·i·sUn_   brown meat from deer. Venison sausages are also available

Vegetables & Staples

arugula [rocket]
ah·ru·gyu·lah
leafy green herb with a slightly bitter taste

baked beans
beikt beens
beans stewed in a sweetened tomato sauce

baked potato
beikt pU·teit·ou
whole potato baked and eaten with skin

cabbage roll
kabitch roul
cabbage leaves stuffed with filling

cilantro _si·lan·trou_
[coriander]
[kO·ree·an·der]
leafy green herb with citrus taste

coleslaw
koul·sloh
sliced cabbage and vegetables in creamy mayonnaise sauce

corn on the cob
korn on dhe cob
fresh corn cooked & eaten on stem

corn Fritter
korn fri·ter
savory fried corn cake

cucumber
kyu·cUm·ber
long green vegetable, often used in salad

eggplant _EgplAnt_
[aubergine]
[ou·ber·djeen]
large purple squash

**fried green
tomatoes** _fraid
green tU·mei·tous_
fried slices of tomato in breadcrumbs

gherkin _gerkin_   small pickled vegetable

mashed potatoes   smooth mashed potatoes, usually served with gravy
pU•tei•tous

sauerkraut   hot pickled cabbage
sauah•kraut

string beans   long, thin green beans
string beenz

spinach *spinitch*   leafy green vegetable, can be eaten raw or
                         cooked

summer squash   tender vegetable, often used in casseroles
sU•mah skwosh

turnip [swede]   white root vegetable, most common in the autumn
tUrnip

tomato   round red fruit often eaten with salad. It has a firm skin
tU•mei•tou [tU•ma•tou]   and is soft and juicy in the centre

Yam [sweet potato]   starchy orange vegetable, often cooked with sugar
sueet pU•tei•tou

Zucchini *su•kee•nee*   long green vegetable with mild taste
[courgette] *[kohrshEt]*

Fruit

apple	*apel*
apricot	*ei•pri•kOt*
banana	*bU•na•na*
black currant	*blak kUrUntkil*
blueberry	*blu•he•ree*
cherry	*tcheree*
fruit	*frut*
grape	*greip*
grapefruit	*greipfrut*
lemon	*lEmUn*
lime	*laim*
melon	*mElUn*
orange	*Orinj*

The U.S. operates on the imperial system of weights and measures. Britain uses both imperial and metric measurements. For example, a supermarket will sell you a **pint** of milk, but most other drinks are packaged as **liters [litres]**. Similarly, you will fill up a car with **litres [U.K.]** or **gallons [U.S.]** of fuel but roadsigns give distances in **miles**.

peach	*peetch*
pear	*pEr*
plum	*plUm*
pineapple	*pain•a•pel*
raspberry	*rasbree*
red currant	*rEd kUrUnt*
strawberry	*strobree*

Cheese

American	mild processed cheese, often comes in slices
ah•mE•ri•kahn	
Cheddar	the most popular English cheese, hard and often yellow
tche•dah	in colour. Comes in various strengths of flavor [flavour].
	Originates from Somerset in the U.K.

YOU MAY SEE...

best if used by...	*bEst if yused bai...*
calories	*kal.e.rees*
fat free	*fat free*
keep refrigerated	*keep ri.frij.e.reit.ed*
may contain traces of...	*mei kUntein treises Ov...*
microwaveable	*mai.krou.weiv.ebel*
sell by...	*sEl bai...*
suitable for vegetarians	*sut.ah.bel for vej.e.tEr.ee.ans*

Cottage Cheese	a soft, textured white cheese that is light and
kO•tidj tcheez	mild in taste
Double Gloucester	a hard cheese from Gloucestershire that is rich and
dabl glohs•tah	buttery. It is orange-red in colour and usually mild
Monterey Jack	mild soft cheese, often used in Mexican dishes
mOn•te•rei djak	

Mozzarella *mO·tsah·rE·lah*	a mild, creamy Italian style cheese
Red Leicester *rEd lEs·tah*	a hard cheese from Leicestershire that is orange-red in colour and usually has a slightly nutty taste
Somerset Brie *sU·mah·set bree*	this is perhaps the most popular soft cheese in the U.K. it is not as rich and strong as French brie
Stilton *stiltn*	a rich and strong tasting blue cheese. There is also white stilton which is milder
Swiss *suis*	mild, nutty cheese with holes
Wensleydale *wEn·zli·deil*	a hard and crumbly white cheese that originates from Yorkshire

Dessert

apple cobbler *apel*	sweet apple filling with crisp pastry top
apple crumble *apl krUmbl*	a baked pudding made from cooked apples and a crumbly mixture of flour, fat and sugar. Served hot
apple pie *apl pai*	a fruit pie of cooked apple and pastry. Served hot often with ice cream or cream
bread and butter pudding *brEd and bU·tah puh·ding*	slices of buttered bread and raisins baked in a mixture of egg, milk and seasoning. Served hot

brownie *braun·ee* rich, fudgy chocolate cake square

cheesecake rich cake made from sweetened cheese with a cookie
tchees·keik base

chocolate fudge cake chocolate sponge cake with rich fudge frosting
tchOklet fUdj keik

Christmas pudding a rich pudding traditionally eaten for dessert at
kris·mas puh·ding Christmas. It contains suet (meat fat), dried fruit, spices
  and brandy. Served hot, often with cream

cookie [biscuit] sweet and crunchy baked treat, often contains
kuhkee [biskit] chocolate or other sweet fillings

cream puffs *kreem* small pastry balls filled with sweet whipped cream

donut [doughnut] fried dough pastry, often coated in a sugary glaze or
dounUt with a sweet filling

Eton Mess a traditional dessert that mixes strawberries with
ee·tn mEs cream and pieces of meringue

fool a dessert that is made from mixing puréed fruit (most
ful often gooseberries) with whipped cream and sugar

hot fudge sundae ice cream served with melted chocolate and
hOt fUdj other toppings

Key lime pie cookie pie crust with lime flavored filling and
kee laim pai meringue top

lemon meringue pie a pastry base with sweet lemon filling and fluffy
lEmUn merang pai meringue top

pumpkin pie sweet pie made from autumnal squash
pUmkin pai

rice pudding a sweet dish made by cooking rice in milk and sugar.
rais puh·ding Served hot. In the UK, jam or cinnamon is often added.

shoofly pie *pai* pie with gooey molasses (treacle/syrup) filling

spotted Dick a hot dessert made from suet (meat fat) and dried fruit
spO·tid dik

summer pudding	a cold sweet dish that combines several soft red and
sU•mah puh•ding	purple fruits
treacle tart	an open pastry filled with golden syrup, breadcrumbs
treekl tArt	and lemon juice. Usually served hot with cream, ice
	cream or custard
trifle	a cold sweet dessert in which a sponge cake is covered
traifl	with fruit or jam and then covered with custard and cream
upside-down cake	a sponge cake that is baked with slices of fruit at the
Up•said•daun keik	bottom and then turned upside down before serving so
	that the fruit is on top

Sauces & Condiments

apple sauce	a sauce or purée made from cooked apples
apl sohs	Traditionally served with pork
barbeque sauce	brown sauce used for grilled meats
bA•bi•kyu sohs	
bread sauce	a milk sauce that is thickened with breadcrumbs
apl sohs	Traditionally served hot with chicken or turkey
chipotle	spicy sauce made from jalapeno peppers
cranberry sauce	a sweet sauce made from cranberries and sugar that is
kran•biri sohs	traditionally served in the UK with turkey at Christmas
English mustard	a thick and spicy yellow sauce. Served cold and usually
ing•lish mUs•tahd	with meat; English mustard is stronger than the French
	or American versions
gravy	a sauce made from the juices of meat that is usually
grei•vee	poured hot over a meat and vegetable dish
horseradish sauce	a strong sharp sauce made from the root of the
hors•radish sohs	horseradish plant. Traditionally served cold with beef
guacamole	thick dip made from avocados
gua•ke•mou•lei	
mint sauce	a sauce made from mint leaves, sugar and vinegar.
mint sohs	Traditionally served with lamb

piccalilli *pi·kah·li·li*	small pieces of preserved vegetables (such as onion and cucumber) mixed into a yellow mustard sauce. The taste is hot like mustard and is often eaten with cold meat
ranch *rantch*	creamy sauce used as a salad dressing or vegetable dip
salsa *sal·sah*	a hot dip of tomatoes, peppers and spices
tartare sauce *tA·tA sohs*	a cold white sauce that is similar to mayonnaise and served with fish. It contains egg and chopped herbs, capers and gherkins
worcestershire sauce *wuhs·tah sohs*	a dark brown spicy sauce containing vinegar, soy sauce and spices

At the Market

Where are the trolleys/baskets?	*wEr Ar dhe trOlees/buskits*
Where is…?	*wEr is…*
I'd like some of that/this.	*aid laik sUm Ov dhat/dhis*

Can I taste it?	*kan ai teist it*
I'd like...	*aid laik...*
a kilo/	
half kilo of...	*ah <u>kee</u>lou/hAlf <u>kee</u>lou Ov...*
a liter of...	*ah <u>lee</u>ter Ov...*
a piece of...	*ah pees Ov...*
a slice of...	*ah slais Ov...*
More/Less	*mor/lEss*
How much?	*hau mUtch*
Where do I pay?	*wEr du ai pei*
A bag, please.	*ah bag, plees.*
I'm being helped.	*aim beein <u>h</u>Elpd*

For Conversion Tables, see page 168.

In the Kitchen

bottle opener	a tool for removing the cork or cap from a bottle
b<u>O</u>tel <u>ou</u>•pen•er	
bowl *boul*	a hollow, round dish for holding food or liquid
can opener	a utensil for opening cans of food
kan <u>ou</u>•pen•er	

YOU MAY SAY...

Do you have any...?	*du yu hav <u>E</u>•nee...*
How much per pound [kilo]?	*hau mUtch pur <u>kee</u>lou [<u>kee</u>lou]*
Give me... kilos [pounds] please.	*Giv mee... <u>kee</u>lous [<u>paunds</u>] plees*
Can I taste it?	*kan ai teist it*

corkscrew _korkskru_   a tool for removing corks from bottles

cup _kUp_   a container to drink from

frying pan _fraiyin pan_   a shallow metal pan with a long handle, in which food is fried

measuring cup/ spoon _mE·shUr·in kUp/spun_   a container for measuring the quantity (usually of a liquid). Mainly used in cooking

napkin _napkin_   a small cloth or piece of paper used to protect clothes while eating

plate _pleit_   a flat dish from which food is eaten or served

pot [saucepan] _pOt [sohs·pahn]_   a container used for cooking, usually made of metal

spatula _spa·tchu·le_   a broad tool used for spreading things in cooking

Eating utensils such as knives, forks and spoons are generically known as **silverware** or **flatware** in the U.S. and are called **cutlery** in the U.K.

Drinks

ESSENTIAL

The wine list/drink menu, please.	*dhe wain list/drink mEnyu, plees*
What do you recommend?	*wUt du yu rE•kU•mEnd*
I'd like a bottle/ glass of red/ white wine.	*aid laik ah <u>bO</u>tel/glAs Ov rEd/wait wain*
The house wine, please.	*dhe haus wain, plees*
Another bottle/ glass, please.	*ahn•<u>U</u>•dhe <u>bO</u>tel/glAs, plees*
I'd like a local beer.	*aid laik ah <u>lou</u>kel beer*
Can I buy you a drink?	*kan ai bai yu ah drink*
Cheers!	*tcheers*
A coffee/tea, please.	*ah kOfee/tee, plees*
Black.	*Blak.*
With...	*wiz...*
cream	*kreem*
milk	*milk*
sugar	*<u>shuh</u>ger*
artificial sweetener	*Ar•ti•<u>fi</u>•shUl <u>suee</u>tner*
A..., please.	*ah..., plees*
juice	*jus*
soda [soft drink]	*<u>sou</u>dah [sOft drink]*
(sparkling/still)	*sp<u>Ar</u>klin/stil <u>woh</u>ter*
water	

Non-alcoholic Drinks

coffee	_kOfee_
hot chocolate	_hOt tchOklet_
lemonade	_lE•mUn•eid_
(sparkling/still)	_(spArklin/stil) wohter_
water	
juice	_jus_
milk	_milk_
(iced) tea	_(aised) tee_

Coffee is the most popular hot drink in the United States and Canada but tea is also drank. **Tea** is the most popular hot drink in the United Kingdom. **Sweetened iced tea** is a common, refreshing cold drink in the hot U.S. summer months.

Tap water is safe to drink and is free of charge in American and British restaurants. **Carbonated soft drinks** are very popular and are called '**soda**' or '**pop**' in different regions (not to be confused with soda water which is a carbonated water!).

YOU MAY HEAR...

Can I get you a drink?	*kan ai gEt yu ah drink*
With milk/cream and sugar?	*wiz milk/kreem and*
	shuhger
Sparkling or still (water)?	*spArklin or stil (wohter)*

Aperitifs, Cocktails & Liqueurs

brandy	*brandee*
gin	*jin*
rum	*rUm*
scotch	*skOtch*
tequila	*te·kee·lah*
vodka	*vOdke*
whisky	*wiskee*

Beer

...beer	*...beer*
bottled/draft	*bOteld/drAft*
[draught]	

Beer is the most popular alcoholic drink among the male drinking population in the U.K and U.S. The most popular kind of British beer is **bitter**, which is dark in color [colour] and served at room temperature. **Lager** is a lighter, golden beer served cold, and is also popular. **Guinness**, which is made in Ireland but enjoyed all over Britain, is very dark and creamy.
The most common style of beer produced by the big breweries in the U.S. is **American lager**.

dark/light	dArk/lait
lager/pilsener	lAger/pilsner
local/imported	loukel/im•port•id
non alcoholic	nOn al•ke•hO•lik

Wine

...wine	...wain
red/white	rEd/wait
house/table	haus/teibel
dry/sweet	drai/sueet
sparkling	spArklin
champagne	shampein
dessert wine	desert wain

Most U.K. pubs close around 11:00 p.m. This has created a culture of going to the pub after work and having drinks with friends or co-workers before going home to eat or dining out. Many pubs offer food too — although the quality can vary greatly. Smoking is not allowed in pubs but many places provide an outdoor area.

On the Menu

angel hair pasta
eindjl hEr pAs•tah
thin spaghetti pasta

baby back ribs
beibee bak ribs
tender beef or pork ribs in a savory sauce

bacon, lettuce & tomato [BLT]
beikUn lEtis and tU•mei•tou
a sandwich containing strips of bacon, lettuce and slices of tomato

baked beans
beikt beenz
haricot beans baked in a tomato sauce

baked potato
beikt pah•tei•tah
a whole potato baked in its skin. The potato is usually cut in two and filled with butter or cheese

bangers and mash
bang•ahz and mash
also known as 'sausages and mash', mashed potato and sausages often served in a gravy sauce

bubble and squeak
bUbl and skweek
a dish made by frying potato and cabbage together. Other vegetables and even meat can be included because this dish is intended to use left-over food from a previous meal (most commonly, the Sunday roast.)

burrito *bah•ri•tou*
Wrap (very flat bread) filled with spicy beans, meat, rice and salsa

cauliflower cheese
koh•li•fla•uer tcheez
cauliflower cooked in a thick white sauce made from cheese. Eaten hot

chicken parmigiana
tchiken
breaded chicken breast covered with tomato sauce and melted cheese, typically served with pasta

chicken tikka massala
tchi•kin•ti•kah mah•sA•lah
chicken in a spicy, creamy orange-red sauce made from yoghurt and tomato. Widely popular

chili [chilli]
chilee
ground meat and beans in a spicy sauce, often served with rice

club sandwich
sAnwitch
double-layered sandwich with turkey, bacon, lettuce and tomato

colcannon
kahl·kan·nahn
an Irish dish that is similar to Bubble and Squeak, containing mashed potato, cabbage and sometimes other vegetables heated together

corn dog
korn dOg
pork sausage fried in corn bread batter

cottage pie
kO·tidj pai
minced beef and vegetables topped with a large layer of mashed potato and baked to form a pie

faggots
fa·gahts
balls of chopped meat, usually pork liver, mixed with herbs and bread. Eaten baked or fried

fajitas
fah·hi·tahz
sizzling meat and peppers in flour wrap (very thin flat bread)

French fries [chips]
frEnch frais
fried slices of potato

game pie
geim pai
a stew containing rabbit, venison or pheasant topped with a thin pastry lid

gravy
grei·vee
a rich brown sauce served with the Sunday roast, made with vegetable juices and stock

gumbo
gUm·bou
hearty stew with meat, spices and vegetables, originally from the Southern U.S.

haggis
ha·gis
a Scottish speciality made from the heart, lungs and liver of a sheep. These are cut up, mixed with suet, onions, oats and seasonings then boiled in a skin made from the sheep's stomach

hamburger
hambUrger
grilled ground beef patty on a roll

homity pie
hO·mi·ti pai
a traditional open vegetable pie in a pastry case usually made from potatoes, onions, leeks and cheese. Dates to world war two when there was a shortage of meat

Irish stew
ai·rish styu
lamb or mutton (meat from a mature sheep) cooked in water with potatoes, onions and often carrots

lasagna *lah·zA·niah*
layered pasta, cheese, meat and tomato sauce

Lancashire hotpot
lan·kah·shah Hot·pOt
lamb or mutton cooked slowly in a pot with onions and sliced potatoes. Other vegetables such as carrots or leek could also be added

macaroni cheese
mah·kah·rou·ni tcheez
pasta in a creamy cheese sauce. Popular in the U.K. and the U.S., where it is known as 'Mac and cheese'

meatloaf
meet·louf
ground beef mixed with herbs baked in loaf pan

mashed potato *masht pah·tei·tah*	potatoes that are boiled and then crushed or 'mashed' until smooth. Butter and milk are usually added
mushy peas *mU·shi peez*	large peas that have been cooked until they form a lumpy green paste, served as part of a traditional fish and chips meal
New York strip steak *steik*	very tender cut of beef, can be cooked from rare to well-done
Philly cheesesteak *tchees·steik*	a roll sliced and filled with thinly cut steak and cheese
pie and mash *pai and mash*	a dish that was most popular in Victorian London. The 'pie' is usually minced beef and pastry. The 'mash' is mashed potato
pizza *peetsa*	round, flat dough covered in tomato sauce and cheese, baked in an oven. Often comes with a choice of vegetable and/or meat toppings
pulled pork sandwich *pUlled pork sAnwitch*	tender pork in smoky sauce on a sliced roll
pork pie *pohk pai*	pastry filled with cooked pork. Often eaten cold as a snack or as part of a larger meal
pickle *pikl*	a chunky and sweet sauce made from vegetables or fruit that have been preserved or 'pickled' in vinegar

Brown in colour, served with cheese

pickled onion
pikld U·niahn

small onions that are preserved or 'pickled' whole in vinegar or salt. Often served with fish and chips

roast potato
roust pah·tei·tah

potatoes roasted in the oven in fat; an essential part of the Sunday roast

spaghetti and meatballs
spU·gE·tee and meet·bawls

pasta served with round balls of beef and Italian herbs in a tomato sauce

shepherd's pie
shep·ahdz pai

lamb mince meat and vegetables topped with a large layer of mashed potato and baked to form a pie

steak and kidney pie
steik and kid·ni pai

a famous British dish consisting of small pieces of beef and the kidney of an ox, lamb or pig in a sauce and covered in pastry

stuffing
stU·fing

stuffing is a filling that is placed inside a piece of meat (or vegetable) before cooking. It often contains breadcrumb, onions and herbs such as sage

Sunday roast
sUn·dei roust

a traditional large family meal eaten on Sundays, now often found in pubs and restaurants. The main ingredient is roasted meat and potatoes. It is served with a variety of other vegetables and gravy

surf n' turf
sUrf•n•tUrf

meal with both meat and seafood

taco *ta•kou*

crunchy corn shell filled with spicy meat and salsa

toad in the hole
toud in dhe houl

sausages cooked in a mixture of eggs, milk and flour. It does not contain toad or frog. Usually served with potatoes and gravy

Yorkshire pudding
yohk•shie puh•ding

a light and fluffy savoury dish made from a mixture of eggs, flour and milk which is traditionally eaten with roast beef

People

ESSENTIAL

What's your name?	*wUts yor neim*
My name is…	*mai neim is…*
Nice to meet you.	*naise tu meet yu*
Where are you from?	*wEr Ar yu frOm*
I'm from the U.K./U.S.	*aim frOm dhe yu-kei/yu-Es*
Can you speak more slowly?	*kan yu speek mor sloulee*
Can you repeat that?	*kan yu ripeet dhat*
What does this/ that mean?	*wUt dUs dhis/dhat meen*
I don't understand.	*ai dount Un•der•stand*
What do you do for a living?	*wUt du yu du for ah living*
I work for…	*ai wUrk for…*
I'm a student.	*aim ah styudent*
I'm retired.	*aim ritaiyerd*
Do you like…?	*du yu laik…*
Goodbye.	*guhdbai*
See you later.	*see yu leiter*

When addressing someone in the U.K. or the U.S., you can say **'Excuse me sir/madam'**, to get their attention, or simply **'Excuse me'** if you do not wish to sound overly formal, especially in the U.S. where people tend to be a bit more casual in their greetings.

Language Difficulties

Can you speak more slowly?	*kan yu speek mor sloulee*
Can you repeat that?	*kan yu ripeet dhat*
Excuse me?	*Ekskyuse mee*
Can you spell it?	*kan yu spEl it*
Please write it down.	*plees rait it doun*
Can you translate this into English for me?	*kan yu transleit dhis intu inglish for mee*
What does this/ that mean?	*wUt dUs dhis/dhat meen*
I understand.	*ai Un·der·stand*
I don't understand.	*ai dount Un·der·stand*
Do you understand?	*du yu Un·der·stand*

YOU MAY SAY...

I can't understand you, can you repeat that?	*ai kant Un·der·stand yu, kan yu ripeet dhat*
Can you spell it?	*kan yu spEl it*
Who are you with?	*hu Ar yu wiz*
Can I have your phone number/e-mail?	*kan ai hav yor (foun) nUmbah/ ee-meil*
Are you on Facebook/ Twitter?	*Ar yu On feisbuhk/tuitah*

Making Friends

Hello!	*hel<u>ou</u>*
Good afternoon.	*guhd Af•ter•<u>nun</u>*
Good evening.	*guhd <u>eev</u>ning*
My name is…	*mai neim is…*
What's your name?	*wUts yor neim*
I'd like to introduce you to…	*aid laik yu tu in•trou•<u>dyuse</u> yu tu…*
Pleased to meet you.	*<u>plee</u>sed tu meet yu*
How are you?	*hau Ar yu*
Fine, thanks. And you?	*fain, tzanks. and yu*

When meeting someone for the first time, it is normal to shake hands in both the United Kingdom and in the United States. It is not the culture to kiss someone you do not know on the cheek. However, people will often smile and say hello to people even if they do not know them, especially in small towns and villages.

Travel Talk

I'm here…	*aim heer…*
on business	*On bisnis*
on vacation [holiday]	*On vei•kei.shUn*
studying	*stUd•ee•ying*
I'm staying for…	*aim steiying*
I've been here…	*aiv been heer beefor*
a day	*ah dei*
a week	*ah week*
a month	*ah mUnz*
Where are you from?	*wEr Ar yu frOm*
I'm from…	*aim frOm…*

For Days, see page 164.

Personal

Who are you with?	*hu Ar yu wiz*
I'm here alone.	*aim heer aloun*
I'm with…	*aim wiz…*
my husband/wife	*mai hUsbUnd/waif*
my boyfriend/ girlfriend	*mai boifrEnd/ girlfrEnd*
a friend	*ah frEnd*
friends	*frEnds*
a colleague	*ah kOleeg*
colleagues	*kOleegs*
When's your birthday?	*wEns yor birzdei*
How old are you?	*hau ould Ar yu*
I'm…	*aim…*
Are you married?	*Ar yu mareed*

I'm...	*aim...*
single/in a relationship	*singel*
engaged	*Engeidjed*
married	*mareed*
divorced	*divorsed*
separated	*sEp•a•reit•ed*
widowed	*widoud*
Do you have children/ grandchildren?	*du yu hav E•nee grand•tchil•dren*

For Numbers, see page 162.

Work & School

What do you do for a living?	*wUt du yu du for ah living*
What are you studying?	*wUt Ar yu stUd•ee•ying*
I'm studying French.	*aim stUd.ee•ying frEnch*
I...	*ai...*
work full-/ part-time	*wUrk fuhl-/pArt-taim*

am unemployed	*am Un•Em-<u>ploid</u>*
work at home	*wUrk at houm*
Who do you work for?	*hu du yu wUrk for*
I work for...	*ai wUrk for...*
Here's my business card.	*heers mai <u>bis</u>nis kArd*

Weather

What's the forecast?	*wUts dhe <u>for</u>kAst*
What beautiful/ terrible weather!	*wUt <u>byu</u>•ti•fuhl <u>wE</u>dher*
It's...	*it's...*

The U.S. climate is mostly temperate, but tropical in Hawaii, Florida and the Deep South; artic in Alaska; semi-arid in the great plains west of the Mississipi River and arid in the Great Basin of the Desert Southwest. Hurricane season, which affects Florida and the Gulf Coast and runs from June 1 to November 30, has produced devastating hurricanes and torrential rain. Tornadoes can strike very suddenly in the Mid-West, even in late winter, if the right conditions arise.

cool/warm	*kul/wohrm*
cold/hot	*kould/hot*
rainy/sunny	*reinee*
snowy/icy	*snouwee*
Do I need a jacket/	*du ai need ah jakEt/*
an umbrella?	*ahn Um•brE•lah*

Romance

ESSENTIAL

Would you like to go out for a drink/dinner?	*wuhd yu laik tu go aut for ah drink/dinah*
What are your plans for tonight/tomorrow?	*wUt Ar yor plans for tUnait/tU.mO.rou*
Can I have your (phone) number?	*kan ai hav yor (foun) nUmbah*
Can I join you?	*kan ai join yu*
Can I buy you a drink?	*kan ai bai yu ah drink*
I love you.	*ai lUv yu*
Please leave me alone.	*plees leev mee aloun*

The Dating Game

Would you like to go out…?	*wuhd yu laik tu go aut…*
for coffee	*for kOfee*

for a drink	*for ah drink*
to dinner	*tu dinah*
What are your plans for...?	*wUt Ar yor plans for...*
today	*tUdei*
tonight	*tUnait*
tomorrow	*tU.mO.rou*
this weekend	*dhis weekEnd*
Where would you like to go?	*wEr wuhd yu laik tu gou*
I'd like to go to...	*aid laik tu gou tu...*
Do you like...?	*du yu laik...*
Can I have your phone number/ e-mail?	*kan ai hav yor foun nUmbah/ee-meil*
Are you on Facebook/Twitter?	*Ar yu On feisbuhk/tuitah*
Can I join you?	*kan ai join yu*
You're very attractive.	*yor vEree ah.trak.tiv*
Let's go somewhere quieter.	*lEts gou sUmwEr kuai.yet.er*

For Communications, see page 46.

Accepting & Rejecting

I'd love to.	*aid lUv tu*
Where should we meet?	*wEr shuhd we meet*
I'll meet you at the bar/your hotel.	*ai-yUll meet yu at dhe bAr/yor houtEl*
I'll come by at...	*ai-yUll kUm bai at...*

I'm busy.	*aim bisee*
I'm not interested.	*aim nOt in.terest.id*
Leave me alone.	*leev mee aloun*
Stop bothering me!	*stOp bOdh.er.ing mee*

For Time, see page 163.

Getting Intimate

Can I hug/kiss you?	*kan ai hUg/kis yu*
Yes.	*yEs*
No.	*nou*
Stop!	*stOp*
I love you.	*ai lUv yu*

Sexual Preferences

Are you gay?	*Ar yu gei*
I'm...	*aim*
heterosexual	*hEt.e.rU.sEk.shu.ahl*
homosexual	*hou.mou.sEk.shu.ahl*
bisexual	*bui.sEk.shu.ahl*
Do you like men/ women?	*du yu lai mEn/wimin*

Leisure Time

ESSENTIAL

Where's the tourist information office?	*wErs dhe <u>tur</u>ist in•for•<u>mei</u>•shUn <u>O</u>ffis*
What are the main sights?	*wUt Ar dhe mein seits*
Do you offer tours in...?	*du yu <u>O</u>fer turs in ...*
Can I have a map/ guide?	*kan ai hav ah map/gaid*

Tourist Information

Do you have information on...?	*du yu hav in•for•<u>mei</u>•shUn On...*
Can you recommend...?	*kan yu rE•kU•<u>mEnd</u>...*
a bus tour	*ah bUs tur*
an excursion to...	*ahn Eks•<u>kUr</u>•shUn...*
a tour of...	*ah tur Ov...*

There are more than 800 Tourist Information Centres (TICs) throughout Britain, which provide free information and advice on local sights, activities and accommodation. Most are open office hours and are generally well-signposted and denoted by a distinctive i symbol. For the U.S., check the website **www.usa.gov** or call 800-FED-INFO for links to government-run tourist information offices for all 50 states.

I'd like to go on the excursion to…	*aid laik tu gou On dhe Eks·kUr·shUn tu…*
When's the next tour?	*wEns dhe nEkst tur*
Are there tours in English?	*Ar dhEr turs in inglish*
Is there an English guide book/ audio guide?	*Is dher ahn inglish gaid buhk/ oh·dee·ou gaid*
What time do we leave/return?	*wUt taim du wee leev/ritUrn*
We'd like to see…	*weed laik tu see…*
Can we stop here…?	*kan wee stOp heer…*
to take photos	*tu teik foutous*
for souvenirs	*for su·ve·neers*
for the toilets	*for dhe toilets*
Is it disabled-accessible?	*is it dis·ei·beld-ak·sE·sibel*

For Tickets, see page 18.

Seeing the Sights

Where's…?	*wErs…*
the battleground	*dhe ba·tel·graund*
the botanical garden	*dhe bO·tan·i·kel gar·den*
the castle	*dhe kasel*
the downtown	*dhe dauntaun*
the fountain	*dhe fauntUn*
the library	*dhe lai·bra·ree*
the market	*dhe markit*

the museum	*dhe myu•zzee•Um*
the old town	*dhe ould taun*
the opera house	*dhe Op•e•rah*
the palace	*dhe palas*
the park	*dhe pArk*
the ruins	*dhe ruins*
the shopping area	*dhe shOpin E•ree•ah*
the town square	*dhe taun skuEr*
Can you show me on the map?	*kan yu shou mee On dhe map*
It's…	*its…*
amazing	*ah•meizz•ing*
beautiful	*byu•ti•fuhl*
boring	*boring*
interesting	*in•terest•ing*
magnificent	*mag•ni•fi•sent*
romantic	*rou•man•tic*
strange	*streindj*
terrible	*tE•ri•bel*
ugly	*Uglee*
I (don't) like it.	*ai dount laik it*

For Asking Directions, see page 32.

Religious Sites

Where's...?	*wErs...*
the cathedral	*dhe ka•tzee•dral*
the Catholic/	*dhe katz•U•lik/prOt•is•tent tchUrtch*
Protestant church	
the mosque	*dhe mOsk*
the shrine	*dhe shrain*
the synagogue	*dhe sin•ah•gOg*
the temple	*dhe tEmpel*
What time is the service?	*wUt taim is dhe servis*

Shopping

ESSENTIAL

Where's the market/mall?	*wErs dhe markit/mohl*
I'm just looking.	*aim jUst luhking*
Can you help me?	*kan yu hElp mee*
I'm being helped.	*aim beeing hElpd*
How much?	*hau mUtch*
That one, please.	*dhat wUn, plees*
That's all.	*dhats ohl*
Where can I pay?	*wEr kan ai pei*
I'll pay in cash/by credit card.	*ai-yUl pei in kash/bai krEdit kArd*
A receipt, please.	*ah riseet, plees*

At the Shops

Where's...?	*wErs...*
the antiques store	*dhe anteeks stOr*
the bakery	*dhe beik•er•ee*
the bank	*dhe bank*
the bookstore	*dhe buhkstOr*
the clothing store	*dhe cloudhing*
the delicatessen	*dhe dEl•i•ka•tE•sen*
the department	*dhe de•pArt•ment*
the gift shop	*dhe gift shOp*
the health food store	*dhe fud stOr*
the jeweler	*dhe juw•el•ler*
the liquor store [off-licence]	*dhe likUr stohr [Off-laisEns]*
the market	*dhe mArkit*
the music store	*dhe myusik stohr*
the pastry shop	*dhe peistree shOp*
the pharmacy	*dhe fAr•mah•see*
the produce [grocery] store [shop]	*dhe prOdyus [grou•se•ree] stohr [shOp]*
the shoe store [shop]	*dhe shu stohr [shOp]*
the shopping mall	*dhe shOping mohl*
the souvenir store [shop]	*dhe su•ve•neer stohr [shOp]*

American stores regularly have sales. British stores also hold sales throughout the year, but January and July are the main ones.

The sales tax system in the United States is quite complicated as it varies from state to state. Some states such as New Jersey do not tax items such as clothing, while groceries and prescription medicine are tax exempt in most states. Where there is a tax to be added, this will be added at the checkout. In the U.K., the price on the tag or label is the price you will pay.

the supermarket	dhe <u>su</u>•per•mAr•kit
the tobacconist	dhe tah•<u>bah</u>•ko•nist
the toy store [shop]	dhe toi stohr [shOp]

Ask an Assistant

When do you open/close?	wEn du yu oupen/klous
the cashier	dhe ka<u>sheer</u>
the escalator	dhe <u>Es</u>•ka•lei•ter
the elevator [lift]	dhe <u>E</u>•le•vei•ter [lift]
the fitting room	dhe <u>fi</u>ting rum
the store [shop] directory	dhe stohr [shOp] di•<u>rek</u>•toh•ree
Can you help me?	kan yu hElp mee
I'm just looking.	aim jUst <u>luh</u>king.
I'm being helped.	aim <u>beeing</u> <u>h</u>Elpd
Do you have...?	du yu have...
Can you show me...?	kan yu shou mee...
Can you ship/wrap it?	kan yu ship/rap it

| How much? | *hau mUtch* |
| That's all. | *dhats ohl* |

For Clothes & Accessories, see page 117.

YOU MAY HEAR...

Can I help you?	*kan ai hElp yu*
One moment.	*wUn moumEnt.*
What would you like?	*wUt wuhld yu laik*
Anything else?	*E•nee•tzing Else*

YOU MAY SEE...

open/closed	*oupen/kloused*
closed for lunch	*kloused for lUntch*
fitting room	*fiting rum*
cashier	*kashccr*
cash only	*kash only*
credit cards accepted	*krEdit kArds aks•sEpt•id*
business hours	*bisnis au•ah*
exit	*Eksit*

Personal Preferences

I'd like something...	*aid laik <u>sUm</u>tzing*
cheap/expensive	*tcheep/Eks•<u>pEn</u>•siv*
larger/smaller	*<u>lar</u>djer/<u>smoh</u>ler*
from this region	*fr<u>O</u>m dhis <u>reedj</u>Un*
Around...dollars/	*a<u>hraund</u>... d<u>O</u>•lahs/paunds/<u>yu</u>rous*
pounds/euros.	
Is it real?	*is it reel*
Can you show me	*kan yu shou mee dhis/dhat*
this/that?	
That's not quite	*dhats n<u>O</u>t kuait w<u>U</u>t ai wahnt*
what I want.	
No, I don't like it.	*nou, ai dount laik it*
It's too expensive.	*its tu Eks•<u>pEn</u>•siv*
I have to think	*ai hav tu tzink abaut it*
about it.	
I'll take it.	*ai-y<u>U</u>l teik it*

Paying & Bargaining

How much?	*hau m<u>U</u>tch*
I'll pay...	*ai-y<u>U</u>l pei...*

in cash	*in kash*
by credit card	*bai krEdit kArd*
by traveler's check	*bai trav•e•lahs tchEk*
A receipt, please.	*ah riseet, plees*
That's too much.	*dhats tu mUtch*
I'll give you...	*ai-yUl giv yu...*
I have only...euros.	*ai hav ounlee yurous*
Is that your best price?	*is dhat yor bEst prais*
Can you give me a discount?	*kan yu giv mee a diskoun*

Checks [cheques] issued by U.S. banks can still be used to pay for goods in stores [shops] in the U.S., but most other English-speaking countries will now only accept payment in cash, by visa, mastercard or debit card.

Traveler's checks are also widely accepted in the U.S. and in the U.K., where they can be used like cash at retail locations, hotels and restaurants. You will need a valid piece of identification to use them.

Making a Complaint

I'd like...	aid laik...
to exchange this	tu Eks·tchEindj
a refund	ah reefund
to see the manager	tu see dhe man·ahdj·er

YOU MAY HEAR...

How are you paying?	hau Ar yu peiying
Your credit card has been declined.	yor krEdit kArd has been diklaind
ID, please.	ai dee, plees
We don't accept credit cards.	wee dount aksEpt krEdit kArds
Cash only, please.	kash ounlee, plees

Both American and British English use decimals rather than commas when writing prices or when communicating fractions of numbers. They symbol for dollars is $ and for pounds sterling is £, followed by the amount (e.g., $20.50, £4.99).

Services

Can you recommend...?	kan yu rE·kU·mEnd...
a barber	ah bArber
a dry cleaner	ah drai-kleener
a hairstylist	ah hEr·stail·ist

a Laundromat	*ah lohn•drou•mat [lohndrEt]*
[launderette]	
a nail salon	*ah neil salUn*
a spa	*ah spA*
a travel agency	*ah travel ei•jen•see*
Can you...this?	*kan yu...dhis*
alter	*ohlter*
clean	*kleen*
fix	*fiks*
press	*prEs*
When will it be	*wEn wil it bee rEdee*
ready?	

Hair & Beauty

I'd like...	*aid laik...*
an appointment	*ahn ah•point•ment for tUdei/tU•mO•rou*
for today/	
tomorrow	
some color/	*seim kUlUr/hailaits*
highlights	
my hair styled/	*mai hEr staild/blou-draid*
blow-dried	

a haircut	ah hErkUt
an eyebrow/	ahn aibrou/
bikini wax	bee•kee•nee waks
a facial	ah feishUl
a manicure/	ah man•i•kyur/pEd•i•kyur
pedicure	
a (sports)	ah (spohrts)
massage	masAdj
A trim, please.	ah trim, plees
Not too short.	nOt tu shohrt
Shorter here.	shohrter heer
Do you offer...?	du yu Ofer...
acupuncture	ak•yu•pUnk•tchtUr
aromatherapy	ah•rou•mah•tzEr•a•pee
oxygen	Oks•i•djen
a sauna	ah sohnah

Antiques

How old is it?	hau ould is it
Do you have	du yu hav
anything from	E•nee•tzing frOm
the...period?	dhe... pi•ree•Ud
Do I have to fill	du ai hav tu fil aut E•nee forms
out any forms?	
Is there a certificate	is dher ah ser•ti•fi•kUt Ov oh•tzEnt•i•si•tee
of authenticity?	
Can you ship/	kan yu ship/rap it
wrap it?	

Clothing

| I'd like... | aid laik... |
| Can I try this on? | kan ai trai dhis On |

YOU MAY HEAR...

What size are you?	*wUt sais ar yu*
How does it fit?	*hau dUs it fit*
Do you need another size?	*du yu need ahn·U·dhe sais*
We don't have your size.	*wee dount hAv yor sais*

It doesn't fit.	*it dUsent fit*
It's too...	*its tu smohl...*
big/small	*big/smohl*

Britain has a thriving fashion market, with its heart in London. Its top designers (including Caroline Charles, Jasper Conran, Katharine Hamnett, Bruce Oldfield, Stella McCartney, Paul Smith and Vivienne Westwood) are the height of haute couture and world-famous. Many top international designers can also be found in London's Knightsbridge and Mayfair.

YOU MAY SEE...

men's	*mEns*
women's	*wimins*
children's	*tchildrins*

short/long	*shohrt/lohng*
tight/loose	*tait/lus*
Do you have this in size...?	*du yu hav dhis in sais...*
Do you have this in a bigger/smaller size?	*du yu hav dhis in ah biger/smohler sais...*

Colors [Colours]

I'd like something...	*aid laik sUmtzing*
beige	*beidj*
black	*blak*
blue	*blu*
brown	*braun*
green	*green*
gray [grey]	*grei*

American and British English sometimes use different spellings of the same word, e.g. color (U.S.)/colour (U.K.), gray (U.S.)/ grey (U.K.), or pajamas (U.S.)/pyjamas (U.K.). However, the pronunciation remains the same.

orange	_Orinj_
pink	_pink_
purple	_pUrpel_
red	_rEd_
white	_wait_
yellow	_yElou_

Clothes & Accessories

a backpack	_ah bakpak_
a belt	_ah bElt_
a bikini	_ah bi•kee•nee_
a blouse	_ah blaus_
a bra	_ah brA_
briefs [underpants] /panties	_breefs [Un•der•pants]/pantees_
a coat	_ah kout_
a dress	_ah drEs_
a hat	_ah hat_
a jacket	_ah jakit_
jeans	_jeens_
pajamas [pyjamas]	_pah•jA•mahs [pi•jA•mahs]_
pants [trousers]	_pants [trausers]_
pantyhose [tights]	_pan•tee•hous [taits]_
a purse [handbag]	_ah pUrs [handbag]_

The word **trousers** (U.K.) and **pants** (U.S.) mean the same thing. Be careful though, in the United Kingdom **pants** is also used to refer to **underwear**. Words for clothing with two legs such as **trousers**, **jeans**, **shorts**, **pajamas**, **pants** and **tights** are always plural in English.

a raincoat	*ah reinkout*
a scarf	*ah skArf*
a shirt	*ah shirt*
shorts	*shohrts*
a skirt	*ah skirt*
socks	*sOks*
a suit	*ah sut*
sunglasses	*sUn•glAs•is*
a sweater	*ah suEtah*
a sweatshirt	*ah suEtshirt*
a swimsuit	*ah swimsut*
a T-shirt	*ah tee-shUrt*
a tie	*ah tai*
underwear	*Un•der•wEr*

Fabric

I'd like...	*aid laik...*
cotton	*kOtUn*
denim	*dEnim*
lace	*leis*
leather	*ledher*
linen	*linen*
silk	*silk*
wool	*wuhl*

| **Is it machine washable?** | *is it mah<u>sheen</u> <u>wahsh</u>•ah•bel* |

Shoes

I'd like...	*aid laik...*
high-heels/flats	*<u>hai</u>-heels/flats*
boots	*buts*
loafers	*<u>lou</u>fers*
sandals	*<u>sandels</u>*
pumps [shoes]	*p<u>U</u>mps [shus]*
slippers	*<u>slipers</u>*
sneakers [trainers]	*<u>sneek</u>ers [<u>trei</u>ners]*
Size...	*sais...*

For Numbers, see page 162.

Women's clothing sizes in the U.S. and U.K. are different. A size 6 in the U.S. is a size 10 in the U.K. As a general rule, for clothing, minus 4 from the U.K. size and for shoes, add 2 to the U.K. size to get the equivalent U.S. size.

Sizes

small (S)	_smohl (Es)_
medium (M)	_meedyum (Em)_
large (L)	_lArdj (El)_
extra large (XL)	_Ekstra lArdj (Eks El)_
petite	_peteet_
plus size	_plUs sais_

Newsagent & Tobacconist

Do you sell foreign-language newspapers?	_du yu sEl for•ain-languitch nyus•pei•pers_
I'd like...	_aid laik..._
candy [sweets]	_kandee [sueets]_
chewing gum	_tchuwing gUm_
a chocolate bar	_ah tchOkelet bAr_
a cigar	_ah sigAr_
a pack/carton of cigarettes	_ah pak/kArtUn Ov sig•a•rEts_
a lighter	_ah laiter_
a magazine	_ah mag•ah•zzeen_
matches	_matchis_

International newspapers are widely available at newsstands, in airports and bus and train stations in major cities in the U.K. and the U.S.

a newspaper	*ah <u>nyus</u>•pei•per*
a pen	*ah pEn*
a postcard	*ah <u>poust</u>kArd*
a road/town map of...	*ah roud/taun map Ov...*
stamps	*stamps*

Photography

I'd like...camera.	*aid laik... <u>kam</u>•e•rah*
an automatic	*ahn oh•tou•<u>mah</u>•tik*
a digital	*ah <u>di</u>•dji•tel*
a disposable	*ah dis•<u>pou</u>•sah•bel*
I'd like...	*aid laik...*
a battery	*ah <u>ba</u>•ter•ee*
digital prints	*<u>di</u>•dji•tel prints*
a memory card	*ah <u>mEm</u>•U•ree kArd*
Can I print digital photos here?	*kan ai print <u>di</u>•dji•tel <u>fou</u>tous heer*

Souvenirs

a bottle of wine	*ah <u>bO</u>tel Ov wain*
a box of chocolates	*ah <u>bO</u>ks Ov tch<u>O</u>kelets*
some crystal	*sUm <u>kris</u>tel*
a doll	*ah dOl*
some jewelry [jewellery]	*sUm <u>ju</u>•wel•ree*

a key ring	*ah kee ring*
a postcard	*ah <u>poust</u>kArd*
some pottery	*sUm <u>pO</u>•ter•ee*
a T-shirt	*ah <u>tee</u>-shirt*
a toy	*ah toi*
Can I see this/that?	*kan ai see dhis/dhat*
I'd like…	*aid laik…*
a battery	*ah <u>ba</u>•ter•ee*
a bracelet	*ah <u>breis</u>let*
a brooch	*ah broutch*
a clock	*ah klOk*
earrings	*ee-ah-rings*
a necklace	*ah <u>nEk</u>lUs*
a ring	*ah ring*
a watch	*ah wahtch*
I'd like…	*aid laik…*
copper	*<u>kO</u>per*
crystal	*<u>kris</u>tel*
diamonds	*<u>dai</u>mUnds*
white/yellow gold	*wait/<u>yE</u>lou*
pearls	*pUrls*

pewter	_pyuter_
platinum	_plat·i·nUm_
sterling silver	_sterling silver_
Is this real?	_is it reel_
Can you engrave it?	_kan yu Engreiv it_

The U.K. offers a wide array of souvenirs. Cloth and wool are probably the most famous speciality, including hand-knitted woollens from Scotland. Nottingham is the traditional manufacturing centre for shoes and lace, and Savile Row in London is the flagship of its bespoke tailoring industry. Famous department stores include Selfridges, Harvey Nichols, Liberty and Harrods. For more light-hearted alternatives, you can also go to the central tourist areas in London like Piccadilly Circus and Leicester Square for an array of souvenir shops full of postcards, gifts and collectables.

In the U.S., New York's famous department stores offer something for almost everyone: the most famous are Bloomingdale's, Lord & Taylor, and Saks Fifth Avenue. Small towns in rural locations and roadside stands are often the most interesting places to find unique souvenirs of the region, from preserved food to handmade clothing and crafts.

Sport & Leisure

ESSENTIAL

When's the game?	*wEns dhe geim*
Where's...?	*wErs...*
the beach	*dhe beetch*
the park	*dhe pArk*
the pool	*dhe pul*
Is it safe to swim here?	*is it seif tu swim heer*
Can I hire clubs?	*kan ai <u>hai</u>-yah klubs*
How much per hour?	*hau mUtch per au-ah*
How far is it to...?	*hau fAr is it tu...*
Can you show me on the map, please.	*kan yu shou mee On dhe map, plees*

Watching Sport

When's...	*wEns...*
(game/race/tournament)?	*(geim/reis/<u>tuhr</u>•nah•ment)*
the baseball	*dhe <u>beis</u>bohl*
the basketball	*dhe <u>bAs</u>•kit-bohl*
the boxing	*dhe <u>bOk</u>sing*
the cricket	*dhe <u>kri</u>ket*
the cycling	*dhe <u>sai</u>kling*
the golf	*dhe gOlf*
the soccer [football]	*dhe <u>sO</u>ker*
the tennis	*dhe <u>tE</u>nis*

the volleyball	*dhe <u>vO</u>•lee•bohl*
Who's playing?	*hus <u>plei</u>ying*
Where's the racetrack/ stadium?	*wErs dhe <u>reis</u>trak/<u>stei</u>dyum*
Where can I place a bet?	*wEr kan ai pleis ah bEt*

For Tickets, see page 18.

Football [soccer] is Britain's most popular spectator and participant team sport. **Rugby**, **golf** and **cricket** are also popular, as well as **tennis**, the Wimbledon Tennis Championship in the summer being one of Britain's best-loved sporting highlights attracting nearly 400,000 spectators worldwide.

The most popular sports in the U.S. are **American football**, **baseball**, **basketball** and **ice hockey**.

What the rest of the world calls **football**, Americans call **soccer**. Americans use the word **football** to mean **American football**.

Playing Sport

Where is/are…?	*wEr is/Ar…*
the golf course	*dhe gOlf kohrs*
the gym	*dhe jim*
the park	*dhe pArk*
the tennis courts	*dhe tEnis kohrts*
How much per…	*hau mUtch per…*
day	*dei*
hour	*au-ah*
game	*geim*
round	*raund*
Can I rent [hire]…?	*kan ai rEnt [hai-yah]…*
some clubs	*sUm klUbs*
some equipment	*sUm i•kuip•ment*
a racket	*ah rakit*

At the Beach/Pool

Where's the beach/ pool?	*wErs dhe beech/pul*
Is there a…?	*is dhEr ah…*
kiddie [paddling] pool	*kidee [padling] pul*

Coastal areas in the U.S. are your best bet for water activities. Deep-sea charters offer fishing activities for grouper, sailfish, and tarpon in Florida and halibut, tuna, and salmon on the Pacific and Northwest coasts. Surfing and swimming predominate along beaches in southern California and to some extent the Atlantic coast. Britain offers plenty of opportunities to those interested in sailing, particularly on the south coast and around Pembrokeshire, southwest Wales. There are also excellent facilities for canoeing, windsurfing, jet skiing and boating too on Britain's many inland waters. Cornwall is a popular surfing centre.

indoor/outdoor pool	*indohr/autdohr pul*
lifeguard	*laifgArd*
Is it safe…?	*is it seif…*
to swim	*tu swim*
to dive	*tu daive*
for children	*for tchildrin*
I'd like to hire…	*aid laik tu hai-yah…*
a deck chair	*ah dEk tchEr*
diving equipment	*daiving i•kuip•ment*
a jet ski	*ah jEt skee*
a motorboat	*ah mou•ter•bout*
a rowboat	*ah roubout*
snorkeling equipment	*snor•kel•ing i•kuip•ment*
a surfboard	*ah sUrfbord*
a towel	*ah tauwel*
an umbrella	*ahn Um•brE•lah*

water skis	*wohter skees*
a windsurfing board	*ah wind·sUrf·ing bord*
For…hours.	*for au-ahs.*

Winter Sports

A lift pass for a day/ five days, please.	*ah lift pAs for ah dei/faiv deis, plees.*
I'd like to hire…	*aid laik tu hai-yah…*
boots	*buts*
a helmet	*ah hElmet*
poles	*pouls*
skis	*skees*
a snowboard	*ah snoubord*
snowshoes	*snoushus*
These are too big/small.	*dheese Ar tu big/smohl*
Are there lessons?	*Ar dhEr lEsUns*
I'm a beginner.	*aim ah be·gin·er.*
I'm experienced.	*aim Eks·pi·ree·Unsd*
A trail map, please.	*ah treil map, plees*

YOU MAY SEE…

lifts	*lifts*
drag lift	*drag lift*
cable car	*keibel kAr*
chair lift	*tcheir lift*
novice	*nOvis*
intermediate	*in·ter·mee·dee·aht*
expert	*Ekspert*
trail [piste] closed	*treil [peest] klousd*

Out in the Country

A map of...,	*ah map Ov..., plees*
please.	
this region	*dhis reedjiUn*
the walking	*dhe wohlking ruts*
routes	
the bike routes	*dhe baik ruts*
the trails	*dhe treils*
Is it...?	*is it...*
easy	*eezzee*
difficult	*di•fi•kUlt*
far	*fAr*
steep	*steep*
How far is it to...?	*hau fAr is it tu...*
I'm lost.	*aim lOst.*
Where's...?	*wErs...*
the bridge	*dhe bridj*
the cave	*dhe keiv*
the desert	*dhe dEsert*
the farm	*dhe fArm*
the field	*dhe feeld*

the forest	*dhe f<u>O</u>rist*
the hill	*dhe hil*
the lake	*dhe leik*
the mountain	*dhe <u>maunt</u>Un*
the nature preserve	*dhe <u>neitch</u>Ur pris<u>er</u>ve*
the viewpoint	*dhe <u>vyu</u>point*
the park	*dhe p<u>A</u>rk*
the path	*dhe p<u>A</u>z*
the peak	*dhe peek*
the picnic area	*dhe <u>pik</u>nik <u>E</u>•ree•a*
the pond	*dhe p<u>O</u>nd*
the river	*dhe river*
the sea	*dhe see*
the (hot) spring	*dhe h<u>O</u>t spring*
the stream	*dhe streem*
the valley	*dhe <u>va</u>lee*
the vineyard	*dhe <u>vin</u>yArd*
the waterfall	*dhe <u>woh.</u>ter•fohl*

ESSENTIAL

What's there to do at night?	*wUts dhEr tu du at nait*
Do you have a program of events?	*du yu hav ah <u>prou</u>gram Ov <u>e</u>vents*
What's playing tonight?	*wUts pleying t<u>U</u>nait*
Where's…?	*wErs…*
the downtown area	*dhe <u>daun</u>taun <u>E</u>•ree•ah*
the bar	*dhe bAr*
the dance club	*dhe dAns klUb*

Entertainment

Can you recommend…?	*kan yu rE•kU•<u>mEnd</u>…*
a concert	*ah <u>kOn</u>sert*
a movie	*ah <u>mu</u>vee*
an opera	*ahn <u>Op</u>•e•rah*
a play	*ah plei*
When does it start/end?	*wEn dUs it start/End*
What's the dress code?	*wUts dhe drEs koud*
I like…	*ai laik…*
classical music	*<u>kla</u>•si•kel <u>myu</u>sik*

folk music	*fouk myusik*
jazz	*jas*
pop music	*pOp myusik*
rap	*rap*

For Tickets, see page 18.

Nightlife

What's there to do at night?	*wUts dhEr tu du at nait*
Can you recommend...?	*kan yu rE•kU•mEnd...*
a bar	*ah bAr*
a cabaret	*ah kab•ah•rei*
a casino	*ah ca•see•nou*
a dance club	*ah dAns klUb*
a gay club	*ah gei klUb*
a jazz club	*ah jas klUb*
a club with French music	*ah klUb wiz frEntch myusik*
Is there live music?	*is dhEr laiv myusik*
How do I get there?	*hau du ai gEt dhEr*

Is there a cover charge?	*is dhEr ah kUver tchArdj*
Let's go dancing.	*lEts gou dAnsing*
Is this area safe at night?	*is dhis E•ree•ah seif at nait*

YOU MAY ASK...

| **Is this area safe at night?** | *is dhis E•ree•ah seif at nait* |
| **Are there any tickets left?** | *Ar dhEr Enee ti•kits lEft* |

Tourist information offices can provide information on local entertainment. Newspapers will usually list upcoming events and events happening that day. In the larger cities, there are magazines and publications that list the local bars, clubs and other venues and activities of interest. These magazines can usually be found in bookstores or at newsstands.

Special Requirements

Business Travel

ESSENTIAL

I'm here on business.	*aim heer On bisnis*
Here's my card.	*heers mai kArd*
Can I have your card?	*kan ai hav yor kArd*
I have a meeting with...	*ai hav a meeting wiz...*
Where's the...?	*wErs dhe...*
business [conference] center	*bisnis [kOn•fe•rens] sEnter*
convention hall	*kUn•vEn•shUn hohl*
meeting room	*meeting rum*

The customary greeting for business people in the U.K and the U.S. is a firm handshake. Last names are usually used instead of first names when meeting someone; say, **Hello, Mr/Mrs...** It is polite to be on time for business meetings.

On Business

I'm here for...	*aim heer for...*
a seminar	*ah sEm•i•nAr*
a conference	*kUn•fe•rens*
a meeting	*ah meeting*
My name is...	*mai neim is...*

May I introduce my colleague... *mei ai in·trU·dyus mai kOleeg...*

I have a meeting/an appointment with... *ai hav ah meeting/ahn ah·point·ment wiz...*

I'm sorry I'm late. *aim sOree*

I need an interpreter. *ai need ahn in·ter·pret·er*

You can contact me at the...Hotel. *yu kan kOntakt mee at dhe... houtEl*

I'm here until... *aim heer Until...*

I need to... *ai need tu...*

    make a call *meik ah kohl*

    make a photocopy *meik ah fou·tou·kOp·ee*

    send an e-mail *sEnd ahn ee-meil*

    send a fax *sEnd ah faks*

    send a package (for next-day delivery) *sEnd ah pakitch (for nEkst dei de·liv·er·ee)*

It was a pleasure to meet you. *it wUs ah pleshUr tu meet yu*

For Communications, see page 46.

YOU MAY HEAR...

Do you have an appointment?	*du yu hav ahn ah·point·ment*
With whom?	*wiz hum*
He/She is in a meeting.	*hee/shee is in ah meeting*
One moment, please.	*wUn moumEnt, plees*
Have a seat.	*hAv ah seet*
Would you like something to drink?	*wUd yu laik sUmtzing tu drink*
Thank you for coming.	*tzank yu for kUming*

Traveling With Children

ESSENTIAL

Is there a discount for kids?	*is dhEr ah diskount for kids*
Can you recommend a babysitter?	*kan yu rE•kU•mEnd ah bei•bee•siter*
Do you have a child's seat/highchair?	*du yu hav ah tchailds seet/haitchEr*
Where can I change my baby?	*wEr kan ai tcheindj mai beibee*

Out & About

Can you recommend something for kids?	*kan yu rE•kU•mEnd sUmtzing for dhe kids*
Where's...?	*wErs...*
the amusement park	*dhe ah•myus•ment pArk*
the arcade	*dhe arkeid*
the kiddie [paddling] pool	*dhe kidee [padling] pul*

YOU MAY SAY...

Can you heat this please?	*kan yu heet dhis plees*
Can I leave the stroller [buggy] here?	*kan ai ah <u>strou</u>ler [<u>bU</u>gee] heer*

the park	*dhe pArk*
the playground	*dhe <u>plei</u>ground*
the zoo	*dhe zzu*
Are kids allowed?	*Ar kids a<u>laud</u>*
Is it safe for kids?	*is it seif for kids*
Is it suitable for... year olds?	*is it <u>sut</u>•a•bel for... yeer oulds*

For Numbers, see page 162.

Baby Essentials

Do you have...?	*du yu hav...*
a baby bottle	*ah <u>bei</u>bee <u>bO</u>tel*
baby food	*<u>bei</u>bee fud*

baby wipes	*beibee waips*
a car seat	*ah kAr seet*
a children's menu/portion	*ah tchildrins menyu/porshUn*
a child's seat/highchair	*ah tchailds seet/haitchEr*
a crib/cot	*ah krib/kOt*
diapers [nappies]	*daipers [napees]*
formula	*for•myu•lah*
a pacifier [dummy]	*ah pas•i•faiy•ah [dUmee]*
a playpen	*ah pleipEn*
a stroller [buggy]	*ah strouler bUgee*
Can I breastfeed the baby here?	*kan ai brEstfeed dhe beibee heer*
Where can I breastfeed/change the baby?	*wEr kan ai brEstfeed/tcheindj dhe beibee*

Babysitting

Can you recommend a babysitter?	*kan yu rE•kU•mEnd ah bei•bee•siter*
How much do you/ they charge?	*hau mUtch du yu/dhei tchArdj*
I'll be back at…	*ai-yUl bee bak at…*
If you need to contact me, call…	*if yu need tu kOntakt mee, kohl…*

Health & Emergency

Can you recommend a pediatrician?	*kan yu rE•kU•mEnd ah pee•dee•ah•tri•shUn*
My child is allergic to…	*mai tchaild is alerdjik tu…*
My child is missing.	*mai tchaild is mising.*
Have you seen a boy/girl?	*hav yu seen ah boi/girl*

Disabled Travelers

ESSENTIAL

Is there…?	*is dhEr…*
access for the disabled	*akses for dhe dis•ei•beld*
a wheelchair ramp	*ah weeltchEr ramp*
a disabled-accessible toilet	*ah dis•ei•beld-ak•sE•si•bel toilet*
I need…	*ai need…*
assistance	*ah•sist•Uns*
an elevator [a lift]	*ahn E•le•vei•ter [ah lift]*
a ground/first-floor room	*ah graund/first-flor rum*

Asking for Assistance

I'm...	aim...
disabled	dis•_ei_•beld
visually impaired	_vi_•su•al•ly imp_Erd_
deaf	dEf
hearing impaired	_heering_ imp_Erd_
unable to walk far/use the stairs	Un•_ei_•bel tu wohlk fAr/yus dhe stErs
Please speak louder.	plees speek _lau_der.
Can I bring my wheelchair?	kan ai bring mai _wee_ltchEr
Are guide dogs permitted?	Ar gaid dOgs per•_mit_•id
Can you help me?	kan yu hElp mee
Please open/hold the door.	plees oupen/hould dhe dohr

In an Emergency

Emergencies

ESSENTIAL

Help!	*hElp*
Go away!	*gou ah<u>wei</u>*
Stop, thief!	*stOp tzeef*
Get a doctor!	*gEt ah <u>dOk</u>ter*
Fire!	<u>*fai-yah*</u>
I'm lost.	*aim lOst*
Can you help me?	*kan yu hElp mee*

In an emergency, dial **999** in the U.K. for police, ambulance or fire brigade. At a hospital, you will need to go to **A&E** (Accident & Emergency).
In the U.S., dial **911**. At a hospital, you will need to go to the **ER** (Emergency Room).

YOU MAY HEAR...

Dial 999. (in the U.K.)	*Dai-yUl nain nain nain*
Dial 911. (in the U.S.)	*Dai-yUl nain wUn wUn*
Is anybody hurt?	*is <u>E</u>•nee bodee hUrt*
Are they conscious?	*Ar dhAy konschuss*
Are they breathing?	*Ar dhAy bree•dhinq*
What is your location?	*wUt is yor <u>louke</u>•shUn*

Police

ESSENTIAL

Call the police!	*kohl dhe pelees*
Where's the police station?	*wErs dhe pelees steishUn*
There was an accident/attack.	*dhErs ahn ak•si•dEnt/atak*
My child is missing.	*mai tchaild is mising*
I need...	*ai need...*
an interpreter	*ahn in•ter•pre•ter*
to make a phone call.	*tu meik ah foun kohl*
I'm innocent.	*aim i•nU•sent*

Crime & Lost Property

I want to report...	*ai wahnt tu repohrt...*
a mugging	*ah mUging*
a rape	*ah reip*
a theft	*ah tzEft*
I was mugged.	*ai wUs mUgd*

YOU MAY HEAR...

Fill out this form.	*fil aut dhis form*
Your ID, please.	*yor ai dee, plees*
When/Where did it happen?	*wEn/wEr did it hapen*
What does he/she look like?	*wUt dUs hee/shee luhk laik*

I was robbed.	ai wUs rObd
I lost…	ai lOst…
…was stolen.	… wUs <u>stou</u>len
My backpack	mai <u>bak</u>pak
My bicycle	mai <u>bai</u>·si·kel
My camera	mai <u>ka</u>·me·rah
My (hire) car	mai (<u>hai</u>-yah) kAr
My computer	mai kUm·<u>pyu</u>·ter
My credit card	mai <u>krE</u>dit kArd
My jewelry	[jewellery] mai <u>ju</u>·wel·ree
My money	mai <u>mU</u>nee
My passport	mai <u>pAs</u>port
My purse [handbag]	mai pUrs [<u>handbag</u>]
My traveler's checks [cheques]	mai <u>trav</u>·el·ahs tchEks
My wallet	mai <u>wah</u>let
I need a police report.	ai need ah pe<u>lees</u> re<u>pohrt</u>
Where is the British/American/Irish embassy?	wEr is dhe <u>bri</u>tish/ah·<u>mEr</u>·i·kan/<u>ai</u>rish <u>Em</u>·bah·see

Health

ESSENTIAL

I'm feeling ill (sick).	*aim feel•in il (sik)*
I need an English-speaking doctor.	*ai need ahn inglish-speeking dOkter*
It hurts here.	*it hUrts heer*

Finding a Doctor

Can you recommend a doctor/dentist?	*kan yu rE•kU•mEnd ah dOkter/dEntist*
Can the doctor come here?	*kan dhe dOkter kUm heer*
I need an English-speaking doctor.	*ai need ahn inglish-speeking dOkter*
What are the office hours?	*wUt Ar dhe Offis au-ahs*
I'd like an appointment for...	*aid laik ahn a•point•ment for...*
today	*tUdei*
tomorrow	*tU•mO•rou*
as soon as possible	*as soon as pO•si•bel*
It's urgent.	*its Urdjent*

Symptoms

I'm bleeding.	*aim bleeding*
I'm constipated.	*aim kOn•sti•peit•id*
I'm dizzy.	*aim dizee*

I'm nauseous.	*aim <u>noh</u>•see•Us*
I'm vomiting.	*aim <u>vOm</u>•it•ing*
It hurts here.	*it hUrts heer*
I have…	*ai hav…*
an allergic reaction	*ahn ah•<u>ler</u>•djik ree•<u>ak</u>•shUn*
chest pain	*tchEst pein*
cramps	*kramps*
diarrhea [diarrhoea]	*dai•ah•<u>reeah</u>*
an earache	*ahn eer eik*
a fever	*ah <u>fee</u>vah*
pain	*pein*
a rash	*ah rash*
a sprain	*ah sprein*
some swelling	*sUm <u>suE</u>ling*
a sore throat	*ah sOr tzrout*
a stomach ache	*ah <u>stUm</u>•ak•eik*
I've been sick for…days.	*aiv been sik for…deis*

For Descriptions, see the Dictionary on page 171.

YOU MAY HEAR...

What's wrong?	*wUts rOng*
Where does it hurt?	*wEr dUs it hUrt*
Does it hurt here?	*dUs it hUrt heer*
Are you on medication?	*Ar yu On mEd•i•kei•shUn*
Are you allergic to anything?	*Ar yu ah•ler•djik tu E•nee tzing*
Open your mouth.	*oupen yor mauz*
Breathe deeply.	*breez deeplee*
Cough, please.	*kOff, plees*
Go to the hospital.	*gou tu dhe hOs•pi•tul*

Conditions

I'm...	*aim...*
anemic	*aneemik*
asthmatic	*asz•mat•ik*
diabetic	*dai•ah•bE•tik*
epileptic	*E•pi•lEp•tik*
I'm allergic to antibiotics/penicillin.	*aim ah•ler•djik tu an•tee•bai•Ot•iks/pEn•i•si•lin*

I have...	ai hav...
arthritis	ar•_tzrai_•tUs
a heart condition	ah hArt KUn•_di_•shUn
high/low blood	hai/lou blUd _prEsh_Ur
pressure	
I'm on...	aim On...

Treatment

Do I need a	du ai need ah pres•_krip_•shUn/_mEd_sin
prescription/	
medicine?	
Can you prescribe a	kan yu pres_kraib_ ah je•_nE_•rik drUg
generic drug?	
Where can I get it?	wEr kan ai gEt it

For Pharmacy, see page 151.

Hospital

Notify my family,	_nou_•ti•fai mai _fam_•i•lee, plees
please.	
I'm in pain.	aim in pein
I need a doctor/nurse.	ai need ah _dOk_ter/nUrs
When are visiting	wEn Ar _vis_•it•ing _au_-ahs
hours?	
I'm visiting...	aim _vis_•it•ing...

Dentist

I have...	ai hav...
a broken tooth	ah _brou_ken tuz
a lost filling	ah lOst _fil_ing
a toothache	ah _tuz_eik
Can you fix this	kan yu fiks dhis _dEntch_Ur
denture?	

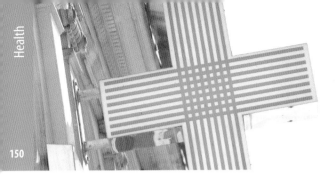

Gynecologist / Gynaecologist

I have cramps/ a vaginal infection.	*ai hav kramps/ah vah•jai•nel in•fEk•shUn*
I missed my period.	*ai misd mai pee•ree•Ud*
I'm on the Pill.	*aim On dhe pil*
I'm (...months) pregnant.	*aim (...mUnzs) prEgnant*
I'm not pregnant.	*aim nOt prEgnant*
My last period was...	*mai lAst pee•ree•Ud wUs...*

For Numbers, see page 162.

Optician

I lost...	*ai lOst...*
a contact lens	*ah kOntakt lEns*
my glasses	*mai glAsis*
a lens	*ah lEns*

Payment & Insurance

How much?	*hau mUtch*
Can I pay by credit card?	*kan ai pei bai krEdit kArd*

| I have insurance. | ai hav in•shuhr•Uns |
| I need a receipt for my insurance. | ai need ah riseet for mai in•shuhr•Uns |

Pharmacy

ESSENTIAL

Where's the pharmacy?	wErs dhe fAr•mah•see
What time does it open/close?	wUt taim dUs it oupen/klous
What would you recommend for…?	wUt wuhd yu rE•kU•mEnd for…
How much do I take?	hau mUtch du ai teik
I'm allergic to…	aim ah•ler•djik tu…

What to Take

How much do I take?	hau mUtch du ai teik
How often?	hau Offen
Is it safe children?	is it seif for tchildrin
I'm taking…	aim teiking…

Boots is the largest chain of chemists [pharmacists] in the U.K., with many branches around the country. As well as selling over-the-counter medicines, they make up prescriptions.
CVS, Walgreen's, Rite Aid and Eckerd's are the biggest pharmacy chains in the U.S., along with Duane Reade in New York. Prescription medication can only be obtained with a doctor's prescription.

Are there side effects?	*Ar dhEr said efekts*
I need something for...	*ai need sUmtzing for...*
a cold	*ah kould*
a cough	*ah kOff*
diarrhea	*dai·ah·reeah*
a headache	*ah hEdeik*
insect bites	*insEkt baits*
motion sickness	*moushUn siknes*
a sore throat	*ah sOr tzrout*
sunburn	*sUnbUrn*
a toothache	*ah tuzeik*
an upset stomach	*ahn UpsEt stOmak*

For Descriptions, see the Dictionary on page 171.

YOU MAY SEE...

once/three times a day	*wUns/tzree taims ah dei*
tablet	*tablet*
drop	*drOp*
teaspoon	*teespun*
on an empty stomach	*On an Emtee stUmak*
swallow whole	*suOlou houl*
may cause drowsiness	*mei kohs drau.si.nes*
do not ingest	*du nOt injEst*

Basic Supplies

I'd like...	*aid laik...*
acetaminophen [paracetamol]	*a•seet•ah•<u>meen</u>•ou•fEn [par•ah•<u>sE</u>•tah•mol]*
antiseptic cream	*an•tee•<u>sEp</u>•tik kreem*
aspirin	*<u>as</u>•pirin*
bandages	*<u>ban</u>•ditchis*
a comb	*ah koumb*
condoms	*kOndOms*
contact lens solution	*kOntakt lens so•<u>lu</u>•shUn*
deodorant	*dee•<u>ou</u>•dU•rUnt*
a hairbrush	*ah <u>hErbrUsh</u>*
hairspray	*<u>hErsprei</u>*
ibuprofen	*ai•byu•<u>prou</u>•fEn*
insect repellent	*<u>insEkt</u> re•<u>pE</u>•lent*
lotion	*<u>loushUn</u>*
a nail file	*ah neil fail*
a (disposable) razor	*ah dis•<u>pous</u>•ah•bel <u>reizer</u>*
razor blades	*<u>reizer</u> bleids*
sanitary napkins [pads]	*<u>san</u>•i•ta•ree <u>napkins</u> [pads]*
shampoo/ conditioner	*shampu/kUn•<u>di</u>•shUn•er*
soap	*soup*
sunscreen	*<u>sUnskreen</u>*
tampons	*<u>tampOns</u>*
tissues	*<u>tishyus</u>*
toilet paper	*<u>toi</u>let peiper*
toothpaste	*<u>tuzpeist</u>*

For Descriptions, see the Dictionary on page 171.

The Basics

Grammar

Simple Present Tense

We use the present tense to talk about general situations or actions. In English, most verbs remain the same as the infinitive when they are conjugated in the simple present tense, but change slightly if the subject is **he**, **she** or **it** by adding **–s** (or **–es**, depending on the spelling of the verb).
Example:
I work for a car company, and David teaches English.
She works in a department store.

In English, the verb **to be** is an irregular verb. Notice that the forms of **to be** are often contracted, or shortened, with the pronouns (I, you, he, she, etc.):

Full Form (Pronoun + Verb)	Contracted Form
I am	I'm
you (sing.) are	you're
he/she is	he's she's
we are	we're
you (pl.) are	you're
they are	they're

Present Continuous Tense

In English the present continuous tense is formed using: **to be (am, is, are) + verb -ing**
Examples:
I am working. / He is going.

We use the present continuous tense to talk about something that is happening exactly at the moment of speaking.

Example:
It's 6:30. We're closing now.

We also use it when something takes place in the present, but not necessarily at the exact moment of speaking.
Example:
Ava has a new job. She's working at a supermarket.

We often use the present continuous tense to talk about a period of time in the present: today, this morning, etc.
Example:
They're having a sale at the department store this week.

Simple Past Tense

The simple past tense usually adds **–ed** to the simple form of regular (and many irregular) verbs. Irregular verbs change in many different ways in the past tense. There are no changes for he, she, or it in any past tense.

We use this tense to talk about completed actions or situations (often brief) that began and ended in the past.
Examples:
John and Kathy went on vacation last week.
William and I saw a great movie on the plane.

It is also used to talk about a frequent action or situation in the past, or a habit that did not continue into the present.
Examples:
Jack drank espresso after dinner every night in Rome.
I slept until 11.00 every morning in college.

Simple Future Tense

There are two forms of the simple future tense:
1. with the auxiliary **will**.
2. with **be** and **going to**.

We use the **will** form to talk about something that will probably happen, future decisions without planning, or a future plan or promise.
Examples:
The train will be late, it always is.
I think we will visit the museum tomorrow.
Andrew and I will bring the wine, as promised.

We use the **to be going to** form to talk about something we are quite sure will happen because of logic, not feelings, and to talk about plans for the immediate or distant future.
Examples:
This isn't going to be an easy test.
We are going to buy a car.

Object Pronouns

These pronouns are used when they are the object of the verb. They receive the action of the verb.
Examples:
He speaks Spanish and Italian, and he speaks them very well.
Where do you teach English? I teach it at the university.
Do you know Susan? Yes, but I don't know her very well.

Subject	Object
I	me
you	you
he	him
she	her

it	it
we	us
you	you
they	them

Word Order

English sentences are constructed as in English: subject, verb, object.
Example: **We're buying a car.**

Questions

English Questions are formed by placing the verb before the subject. Note
below that this is the opposite of the statement, where the subject comes
before the verb:

Statements	Questions
You are from Liverpool.	**Are you from Liverpool?**
He is from Canada.	**Is he from Canada?**

Negations

To make a verb negative, you use the following construction:
I/you/they + **do not** + verb   he/she/it + **does not** + verb

In spoken English, these forms are usually contracted to: **don't, doesn't.**
Examples:
I don't work for a car company. = I do not work for a car company.
She doesn't teach French. = She does not teach French.
The hotel doesn't have a nice restaurant.

Articles

In English, nouns are preceded by either definite or indefinite articles. The
indefinite article **(a/an)** is used to refer to a noun in a general sense. It can
often be replaced by the number **one**.
The English indefinite article has two forms, **a** and **an**:

You use **a** before a consonant sound.
Examples:
I'd like a hamburger, please.
I'll have a tuna sandwich.

You use **an** before a vowel sound.
Example:
I'd like an orange juice.
It's an MP3 player. (MP3 is pronounced '*em•pee•three*')

The definite article (**the**) is used to refer to a specific noun, about one specific noun in a general group, or about a specific noun that the speaker and listener both recognize.
Examples:
Who is driving the car? (our car)
Peter is the boy with red hair. (no other boy in the group has red hair)
How would you like the steak sir? Medium? (the steak the man asked for)

Adjectives

In English, adjectives usually come before the word they describe.
Examples:
Do you have any cheap cameras?
Two black T-shirts, please.

Good or Well?

Good is an adjective (an adjective describes a noun). **Well** is an adverb (an adverb describes a verb).
Examples:

He speaks good Chinese.	**He speaks Chinese well.**
Your Polish is good.	**You speak it well.**
She's a good reader.	**She reads well.**

Possessive Adjectives

Possessive adjectives show that an object belongs to someone or something:
His name is Tom.   That's **my** coffee!   **Her** name is Susan.

Subject	Possessive Adjective
I	*my*
you	*your*
he	*his*
she	*her*
it	*its (animal or object)*
we	*our*
you (plural)	*your (plural)*
they	*their*

Note: The third person (his/her) agrees with the gender of the possessor.
Examples:
Paul took **his** suitcase. **(Paul is masculine.)**
Susan took **her** suitcase. **(Susan is feminine.)**

To show possession, add **'s** to a person's name.
Example: Judy's last name is Wells.

Prepositions

By
Examples: **How do you get to work? By bus.**
She goes to work by taxi.

On
Example: **Do you come to work on foot?**

To
Verbs such as **to work, to come, to go, to drive,** and **to ride** are followed by
to + a location:

How do you come to work?
They ride the subway [underground].
He drives to the station.
She goes to school.

Note that **home** is an exception. We don't use a preposition with expressions such as **get home, go home, come home** and **drive home.**
Examples:
How do you get home?
They go home on foot.
Does he drive home?

For
Examples: **I wait for the train at the station.**
I'm waiting for the subway [underground].

Prepositions of Time

We use **at** when we talk about something that happens at a specific time.
Examples:
The store opens at 9:15.
I'm sorry, but this restaurant closes at midnight.

From and **to** indicate a period of time.
Examples:
The market is open from 8:00 a.m. to 6:00 p.m.
We're open from Monday to Friday.

We use **on** with the days of the week.
Examples:
We're open on Saturdays, but we're closed on Sundays.
Note that in this example the day of the week is plural. This is because we are talking about something that happens regularly.

Word Stress

The stressed syllable in a word is the syllable that you hear as being the loudest and longest.

Say the word **number**. Notice that the syllable *'num'* is louder and longer than *'ber.'* Though many English words follow a stressed-unstressed pattern, like **number**, it is not always easy to guess where the stress falls in an English word.

Pronunciation

When Americans in particular speak quickly or informally, unemphasized words, or words that do not receive stress, become reduced. That is, the vowel sounds are not as long, and some consonants (such as initial **h**) reduce or even disappear. This is often the case with pronouns that begin with **h**.
Examples:

I see'im! = **I see him!**

Do you trust'er? = **Do you trust her?**

Spellings

In some cases, American and British English use different spellings. For example, the American English word **color** is spelled [spelt] **colour** in British English (similar examples are **theater/theatre, favorite/favourite, neighbor/neighbour**). However, some of these differences are irregular and can only be learned. For example, the noun **practice** is the same in both American and British English, but the verb is **practice** in American English and **practise** in British English.

Different tenses of certain words are also spelled [spelt] differently. For example, the past tense of **travel** is **traveled** in American English but **travelled** in British English. Words like **recognize** have **z** endings in American English but in British English, both **z** or **s** can be used (**recognize/recognise**).

Numbers

ESSENTIAL

0	*zero*	*zzeerou*
1	*one*	*wUn*
2	*two*	*tu*
3	*three*	*tzree*
4	*four*	*fohr*
5	*five*	*faiv*
6	*six*	*siks*
7	*seven*	*sEven*
8	*eight*	*eit*
9	*nine*	*nain*
10	*ten*	*tEn*
11	*eleven*	*ee•lEv•en*
12	*twelve*	*tuElve*
13	*thirteen*	*tzirteen*
14	*fourteen*	*fohrteen*
15	*fifteen*	*fifteen*
16	*sixteen*	*siksteen*
17	*seventeen*	*sEv•en•teen*
18	*eighteen*	*eiteen*
19	*nineteen*	*nainteen*
20	*twenty*	*tuEntee*
21	*twenty-one*	*tuEntee-wUn*
22	*twenty-two*	*tuEntee-tu*
30	*thirty*	*tzirtee*
31	*thirty-one*	*tzirtee-wUn*
40	*forty*	*fohrtee*
50	*fifty*	*fiftee*

60	sixty	_sikstee_
70	seventy	_sEv•en•tee_
80	eighty	_eitee_
90	ninety	_naintee_
100	one hundred	wUn _hUn_dred
101	one hundred and one	wUn _hUn_dred and wUn
200	two hundred	tu _hUn_dred
500	five hundred	faiv _hUn_dred
1,000	one thousand	wUn _tzau_sand
10,000	ten thousand	tEn _tzau_sand
1,000,000	a million	ah _mily_Un

Ordinal Numbers

first	_ferst_
second	_sEk_Und
third	_tzird_
fourth	_fohrz_
fifth	_fifz_
once	_wUns_
twice	_tuais_
three times	_tzree taims_

Time

ESSENTIAL

What time is it?	_wUt taim is is_
It's midday.	_its mid•dai_
At midnight.	_at midnait_
From one o'clock	_frOm wUn ah-klOk tu tu ah-klOk_
to two o'clock.	

Five past three.	*faiv pAst tzree*
A quarter to ten.	*ah kuArter tu tEn*
5:30 a.m./p.m.	*faiv ei Em/pee em*

Use **in** to talk about time: in the morning, in the afternoon, in the evening.

It's 3:00 (three o'clock) in the morning.

Is it 7:00 (seven o'clock) in the evening?

In also shows location: a city or country.

What time is it in Tokyo?

It's 5:00 (five o'clock) in Rome.

In United Kingdom and in the United States, people mostly use the 12-hour clock (from 1 to 12) to give the time. 18:35 = 6:35 (six thirty-five p.m.). To tell if someone is talking about time in the morning or in the afternoon, add the abbreviation **a.m.** for times between midnight and noon. For times between noon and midnight, add the abbreviation **p.m.** When it is obvious in context what time is meant, you can simply say **It's one o'clock, It's two o'clock**, etc.

Days

ESSENTIAL

Monday	*mUndei*
Tuesday	*tchusdei*
Wednesday	*wEnsdei*
Thursday	*tzUrsdei*
Friday	*fraidei*
Saturday	*sat•er•dei*
Sunday	*sundei*

yesterday	_yEs_•ter•dei
today	tU_dei_
tomorrow	tU•_mO_•rou
day	dei
week	week
month	mUnz
year	yeer

In the U.S., calendars are organized Sunday to Monday. In U.K., they are organized Monday to Sunday.

Months

January	_jan_•yu•a•ree
February	_fEb_•ru•a•ree
March	mArtch
April	_ei_pril
May	mei
June	jun
July	ju_lai_
August	_ohg_Ust
September	sEp•_tEm_•ber
October	Ok•_tou_•ber
November	nou•_vEm_•ber
December	di•_sEm_•ber

The U.S. follows a month-day-year format to express the date, whereas the U.K. favors [favours] a day-month-year format.
Example: July 25, 2008 = 07/25/08 in the U.S.
25 July, 2008 = 25/07/08 in the U.K.

Seasons

spring	*spring*
summer	*sUmer*
autumn	*ohtUm*
winter	*winter*

Holidays

Official Public Holidays

January 1: New Year's Day *nyu yeers dei*

May 1: Labor Day (U.S) *leibor dei*

May 8: Victory Day (U.S) *vik•te•ree dei*

July 4: Independence Day (U.S) *in•di•pEn•dens dei*

November 1: All Saints Day *ohl seints dei*

In the United States, important holidays are New Year's Day (1st
January), Independence Day, (4th July), Thanksgiving (the 4th
Thursday in November) and Christmas Day (25th December).
In the United Kingdom, important holidays are New Year's Day,
Christmas and Boxing Day (25th-26th December) plus Bank Holidays
(these are always Mondays but the dates change every year).

November 11: Armistice Day _Ar•mis•tis dei_
December 25: Christmas Day _krismas dei_
December 26: Boxing Day (U.K.) _bOksing dei_

Moveable Feasts/Holidays
Good Friday _guhd fraidei_
Easter Sunday _eester sUndei_
Easter Monday _eester mUndei_
Martin Luther King Day (U.S) _MArtin luzer king dei_
President's Day (U.S) _prEs•i•dents dei_
Veterans' Day (U.S) _vEt•er•rUns dei_
Thanksgiving Day (U.S) _tzanks•giv•ing dei_
Memorial Day (U.S) _me•mor•ree•ahl dei_
Columbus Day (U.S) _kU•lUm•bUs dei_
Ascension _a.sEn.shUn_
Pentecost _pEn.ti.kOst_

Conversion Tables

When you know	Multiply by	To find
ounces *aunsis*	*28.3*	grams *grams*
pounds *paunds*	*0.45*	kilograms *ki·lah·grams*
inches *intchis*	*2.54*	centimeters *sEn·ti·mee·ters*
feet *feet*	*0.3*	meters *meeters*
miles *mails*	*1.61*	kilometers *ki·lO·mit·ers*
square inches *skuEr intchis*	*6.45*	sq. centimeters *skuEr sEn·ti·mee·ters*
square feet *skuEr feet*	*0.09*	sq. meters *skuEr meeters*
square miles *skuEr mails*	*2.59*	sq. kilometers *skuEr ki·lO·mit·ers*
pints (U.S./U.K.) *paints*	*0.47/0.56*	liters *leeters*
gallons (U.S./U.K.) *galUns*	*3.8/4.5*	liters *leeters*
Fahrenheit *fa.ren.hait*	*5/9, after −32*	Centigrade *sEn·ti·graid*
Centigrade *sEn·ti·greid*	*9/5, then +32*	Fahrenheit *fa·ren·hait*

Kilometers [kilometres] to Miles Conversions

1 km *wUn ki·lO·mit·er*	0.62 miles *seerou point siks tu mails*
5 km *faiv ki·lO·mit·ers*	3.1 miles *tzree point wUn mails*
10 km *tEn ki·lO·mit·ers*	6.2 miles *siks point tu mails*
50 km *fiftee ki·lO·mit·ers*	31 miles *tzirtee-wUn mails*
100 km *wUn hUndrid ki·lO·mit·ers*	62 miles *sikstee-tu mails*

Measurement

1 gram	= 1000 milligrams	= 0.035 oz.
wUn gram	*wUn tzausand mi·li·grams*	*seerou point seerou tzree faiv aunsis*
1 kilogram (kg)	= 1000 grams	= 2.2 lb
wUn ki·lah·gram	*wUn tzausand grams*	*tu point tu paunds*
1 liter (l)	= 1000 milliliters	= 1.06 U.S./0.88 U.K. Quarts
wUn leeter	*wUn tzausand mi·li·lee·ters*	*wUn point seerou siks yu Es/ seerou point eit eit bri·tish kuohrts*
1 centimeter (cm)	= 10 millimeters	= 0.4 inch
wUn sEn·ti·mee·ter	*tEn mi·li·mee·ters*	*seerou point fohr inchis*
1 meter (m)	= 100 centimeters	= 39.37 inches/3.28 ft.
wUn meeter	*wUn hUndrid sEn·ti·mee·ters*	*tzirtee-nain point tzree sEven inchis/tzree point tu eit feet*
1 kilometer (km)	= 1000 meters	= 0.62 miles
wUn ki·lO·mit·er	*wUn tzausand meeters*	*seerou point siks tu mails*

Temperature

-40°C – -40°F	**-1°C** – 30°F	**20°C** – 68°F
-30°C – -22°F	**0°C** – 32°F	**25°C** – 77°F
-20°C – -4°F	**5°C** – 41°F	**30°C** – 86°F
-10°C – 14°F	**10°C** – 50°F	**35°C** – 95°F
-5°C – 23°F	**15°C** – 59°F	

Oven Temperature

100°C – 212°F	**177°C** – 350°F
121°C – 250°F	**204°C** – 400°F
149°C – 300°F	**260°C** – 500°F

the left hand a

ng towards, or
r its principles
ongs to the political

a place at a railway
uggage may be left for
ndant for safekeeping.
eckroom
en plural) an unused
material or of cooked
sed portion or remnant
es or towards the left

afterward adv towards

legally adv

legal aid n a means-tested benefit in the form of ... assistance for persons to meet the cost ... advice and representation in legal proceedings

legal cap n US ruled writing paper, about 8 by 13½ inches with the fold at the top, for use by lawyers

legalese (li:gə'li:z) n the conventional language in which legal documents, etc., are written

legal holiday n US any of several weekdays ... called (Canadian) **statutory holiday**. Also ...

legend

A

abbey *n* a building where monks or nuns live or lived

accept *v* to agree to take (something offered); to acknowledge

access *v* to gain entry to a place or information from a computer or telephone

accident *n* an unexpected event or incident, often with unfortunate results; a vehicle crash

accommodations (U.S.), accommodation (U.K.), *n* the place where someone lives when they are on holiday or working away from home

account *n* an amount of money deposited at a bank

acupuncture *n* medical treatment in which needles are stuck into the skin at specific points to relieve pain or cure disease

adapter (U.S.), adaptor (U.K.) *n* a device for connecting an electrical plug to a socket

address *n* the name of the place where a person lives or where a building is located

admission *n* the act of entering a place or building

aeroplane (see airplane)

after *adv, prep., conj.* following (in time or sequence)

afternoon *n* the time between midday and evening

aftershave *n* a lotion applied to the face after shaving to make you smell good

age *n* the number of years someone has lived

agency *n* a person or business that provides a service, such as a travel agent

AIDS *n* a condition caused by the HIV virus which attacks the body's immune system, leaving it defenceless against disease

air *n* the invisible gases surrounding the earth; the substance required for breathing

abbr abbreviation	**conj** conjunction	**v** verb
adj adjective	**n** noun	**U.S.** American English
adv adverb	**prep** preposition	**U.K.** British English

air-conditioning *n* a system for cooling or controlling the temperature in a room or building

air-pump *n* an instrument for putting air into an object like a ball or tire

airline *n* a commercial organization operating regular transport by air

airmail *n* mail transported by aircraft

airplane (U.S.), aeroplane (U.K.) *n* a flying vehicle that transports people or goods through the air

airport *n* a place where passenger and freight airplanes take off and land

aisle *n* a passage between the seats in a place (such as in a theater or on an airplane)

aisle seat *n* the chair directly next to the aisle on an airplane

allergy *n* a severe negative response or reaction by the body to a food or substance

allow *v* to say that it is okay for somebody to do something

alone *adj* all by yourself with no one else present

alter *v* to change or modify something

alternate *adj* other possible (such as *take an alternate route*)

aluminum foil (U.S.), aluminium foil (U.K.) *n* a roll of thin metal sheet used to wrap food

amazing *adj* very good (such as in *an amazing view*)

ambulance *n* a vehicle for transporting sick or injured people to hospital

American *adj* relating to a person or thing from America (the continent) or the U.S.A. *n* a person from the U.S.A.

amusement park *n* a place for pleasure, containing rides and attractions

anemic *adj* suffering from anemia, a blood condition which makes the person pale and tired

anesthetic (U.S.), anaesthetic (U.K.) *n* the substance that removes the feeling of pain during a medical procedure

animal *n* a living creature that is not a human being, insect, bird, or fish

ankle *n* the joint between the foot and the leg

antibiotic *n* a medicine (such as penicillin) that destroys infectious bacteria

antique *n* an old item such as art or furniture which people collect

antiques store *n* a shop selling antiques

antiseptic cream *n* an ointment or lotion that helps prevent infection

anything *n*, *pron.* referring to any thing or object

apartment *n* a separate room or collection of rooms in a building where a person or people live

appendix *n* an internal organ which has no real use and can be removed if infected

appetizer (U.S.), **appetiser (U.K.)** *n* food or drink served before or at the beginning of a meal

appointment *n* a meeting or arrangement scheduled for a specific time (such as *a doctor's appointment*)

arcade *n* a covered passage with shops on each side

area code *n* a number used before a phone number in a different part of the country

arm *n* the upper limb of the human body on either side, from the shoulder to the hand

aromatherapy *n* the use of massage with essential plant oils

around (U.S.), **round (U.K.)** *prep* on the other side of (such as *around the corner*)

arrivals *n* the area at an airport for passengers who have just arrived on a flight

arrive *v* to get to or reach a place or destination

artery *n* one of the body's major blood vessels

arthritis *n* painful inflammation of joints in the body that causes stiffness

art *n* creative works, such as paintings or sculptures

Asian *adj* relating to a person or thing from the continent of Asia. *n* a person from Asia

Aspirin® *n* a tablet used to give relief from pain

asthma *n* a medical disorder that makes breathing difficult

ATM *(abbr.)* automated teller machine; *n* a machine for withdrawing money from a bank account

ATM card *n* a plastic card required to operate a cash machine

attack *n* a violent assault or injury by a person

attend *v* to go to an event or meeting

attraction *n* a place (or thing) that people go to see

attractive *adj* nice to look at

Australian *adj* relating to a person or thing from Australia. *n* a person from Australia

automatic *adj* relating to something that works by itself

automatic car *n* a vehicle that changes gear by itself, without human operation

available *adj* able to be used or accessed

B

baby *n* an very young child that cannot walk or speak yet

baby bottle *n* a bottle used for giving milk to a baby

baby wipe *n* a tissue used for cleaning a baby

baby-sitter *n* a person who looks after a child while the parents are not there

back *n* the rear part of the human body, from the shoulders to the hips

backache *n* pain in a person's back

back-pack *n* a bag carried on a person's back

bag *n* flexible container, used for putting in and carrying objects, often when shopping

baggage *n* bags and cases carried when traveling

baggage claim *n* the area in an airport where passengers collect their luggage after getting off the plane

baggage ticket *n* the receipt given for cases that (usually at an airport)

bakery *n* a place where bread and cakes are made or sold

ballet *n* a performance in which a stor is told through dance and music

bandage *n* a strip of flexible material used to bind up wounds

bank *n* a place where people deposit, invest and withdraw money

bar *n* a place where alcoholic drinks are served and drunk

barbecue *n* a meal at which food is prepared outdoors over a charcoal fir

barber *n* a person who shaves and cut beards and hair

baseball *n* the national ballgame of America; the ball used in the game

basket *n* a container used for carrying items, usually when shopping

basketball *n* a popular sport where teams score points by throwing a bal through a hoop; the ball used in the game.

bathroom *n* a room containing a toilet and washbasin, and/or a bath or shower

battery *n* an object (usually small and portable) that provides power to an electrical device

battleground *n* the site of a famous historic war or battle

beach *n* an area of sand or small stone on the edge of the sea or a lake

beautiful *adj* attractive to the eye or senses

bed *n* a piece of furniture for sleeping on

bed and breakfast *n* a small hotel or private house that provides overnight accommodation with breakfast

before *prep* in front of or prior to an object, time or action

begin *v* to start; to do first

beginner *n* someone who is doing something for the first time; someone who is inexperienced at a particular skill or activity

behind *prep* at the back of something; after an object (such as *behind a person in a line*); after a time or action

belt *n* a flat strip of material (often leather) that fastens around the waist to support trousers or other clothing

berth *n* a bed on board a ship or train; a place for boats to be tied up

best *adj* of the highest quality; surpassing all others; most desirable

better *adj* superior; more desirable; improved in health

bicycle *n* a two-wheeled vehicle which is driven by pedals

big *adj* large or great in bulk

bigger *adj* larger or greater than another object

bike route *n* a path or track specifically for the use of people on bicycles

bikini *n* a small, two-piece swimming costume

bikini wax *n* the removal of pubic hair through using wax

bill *v* to charge an amount of money for goods or services; *n* a piece of paper showing the amount of money owed for goods or services (often in a restaurant); a note of currency (such as a dollar bill)

bird *n* a creature with wings and feathers that can usually fly

birthday *n* the anniversary of the day a person was born

black *adj* intensely dark in color

bladder *n* internal organ which holds urine until it is passed out of the body

bland *adj* dull; lacking in strong flavors

blanket *n* a covering for for a bed, often made of wool

bleed *v* to lose blood, especially when injured

blood *n* the red liquid that circulates through the veins

blood pressure *n* the pressure of blood flowing through the veins, measured as an indicator of health

blouse *n* a shirt for women

blue *adj* of the color of the cloudless

board *v* to get onto a vehicle (such as a bus, train, ship or airplane)

boarding pass *n* a ticket authorising a person to board an airplane or other form of transport

boat *n* a vessel that travels on water (usually smaller than a ship)

bone *n* a piece of the hard material that forms the skeleton of the body

book *n* a printed set of pages held together by a cover

bookstore *n* a shop selling books

boots *n* shoes (usually made of leather) that cover the foot and part of the leg

boring *adj* dull, uninteresting

botanical garden *n* a large public garden laid with many plants which are studied scientifically

bother *v* to annoy or pester

bottle *n* a container with a narrow neck for holding liquids (usually made of glass or plastic)

bottle opener *n* a tool for removing the cork or cap from a bottle

bowl *n* a hollow, round dish for holding food or liquid

box *n* a flat-sided square or rectangular container for carrying or storing items

boxing match *n* a sporting event where two people fight in a ring

boy *n* a male child

boyfriend *n* a male partner with whom a woman or man has a romantic or sexual relationship

bra *n* an item of underwear worn by females to support the breasts

bracelet *n* a ring or band worn on the wrist or arm for decoration

brakes *n* the appliance used to slow down or stop a vehicle

break *v* to separate an item into pieces by force; to fracture (such as in *to break an arm*)

breakdown *n* the mechanical failure of a vehicle

breakfast *n* the first meal of the day

break-in *n* a forced entry or burglary of a property or vehicle

breast *n* either of the two organs on a woman's chest

breastfeed *v* to feed a baby from the breast instead of the bottle

breathe *v* to take air into the lungs or let it out

bridge *n* a structure for crossing over a river or other obstacle

briefs *n.pl.* close fitting underpants

bring *v* to take along with (an object or person)

British *adj* relating to a person or thing

from Britain

broken *adj* in pieces; not working

brooch *n* an ornamental clasp with a pin, for fastening clothing

broom *n* a long-handled brush used for sweeping

brother *n* a son of the same parents as another son or daughter

brown *adj* a color [colour] of dark wood

bug *n* an insect of any variety

building *n* a structure such as a house where people live or work

burn *v* to destroy something by fire

bus *n* a long road vehicle that carries many passengers

bus station *n* the place where buses begin and end their journeys

bus stop *n* a place marked by a sign at which buses stop to pick people up or let them off passengers

bus ticket *n* a piece of paper that entitles a passenger to make a journey on a bus

bus tour *n* an organised bus journey for tourists, usually with a guide

business *n* a commercial organisation, company or establishment; a person's affairs or activities (such as in *to go about your own business*)

business card *n* a card printed with a company's name, address and phone number, and the identity of the person who carries it

business center (U.S.), **business centre** (U.K.) *n* a place in a hotel or airport with facilities for people to work when they are traveling, usually containing computers, phone and internet facilities

business class *n* a section of seating and service on an airplane or other form of transport that is superior to economy class

business hours *n* fixed hours of work or opening times in a shop, office etc (often 9:00am to 5:00pm)

butcher *n* a shop specialising in selling fresh meat; the person who works in such a shop

buttocks *n.pl.* the two rounded parts of the body that humans sit on

buy *v* to give money in return for a product or service

bye *int coll* informal term for goodbye

C

cabaret *n* entertainment consisting of singing, dancing etc; a restaurant or nightclub where such entertainment is provided

cabin *n* a room or compartment in a

ship or aircraft for passengers; a small hut or house (such as *a log cabin*)

cable car *n* a vehicle suspended from a thick overhead wire, usually used for traveling up and down mountains or across ravines

cafe *n* a small restaurant where you can buy and have light meals and drinks

call *v* to contact and speak to someone through a telephone; to give a name to

call collect *n* a telephone call for which the person who answers the call pays the charges

calorie *n* a unit measuring the energy content of food, often provided as part of dietary information

camera *n* a device for taking photographs

camera case *n* a small case to protect a camera when it is not being used

camp *v* to sleep outdoors in a tent

camping stove *n* a portable cooker, usually gas-powered

campsite *n* a place set aside, or suitable, for camping

Canadian *adj* relating to a person or thing from Canada

cancel *v* to decide or declare that something will not take place as

planned; to make a ticket or booking invalid

candy (U.S.) *n* sweet food made with sugar and often containing chocolate, nuts, fruits etc

canned goods *n* foods stored or contained in a can

can opener *n* a utensil for opening cans of food

canyon *n* a deep gorge or ravine with steep sides

car *n* a road vehicle with a motor and (usually) with four wheels for a small number of people

car hire *n* paying money to use a car for a limited period

car park *n* a place where cars may be left for a limited period

car rental (see car hire)

car seat *n* a chair used for transporting children or babies securely in a car

carafe *n* a glass jar for holding wine or water at table

card *n* a small rectangular piece of plastic (or sometimes stiff paper) containing personal information or credit; a thick piece of paper containing a message or greeting (such as a birthday card)

carry-on *n* a small piece of hand luggage you are allowed to take with you on an aircraft

cart *n* a vehicle with two wheels and no roof which transports heavy goods; a a large shopping basket on four wheels in a supermarket or store

carton *n* a box for holding liquids or other items, usually made from cardboard or plastic

carton of cigarettes *n* a box containing packs of cigarettes

case1 *n* a container designed to hold or protect an object or objects

case2 *n* an event or circumstance (such as *it is a case of*)

cash *n* money in coin or note form *v* to turn into or exchange for cash

cash advance *n* money given ahead of scheduled payment; money transferred from another source

cashier *n* a person who handles payments in a shop or business

casino *n* an establishment where people go to gamble (usually containing games such as roulette, blackjack, slot machines etc)

castle *n* an old, very strong building, often on a hill, which was easy to defend against attack

cathedral *n* a very large church

cave *n* a hollow place in the earth or rocks

CD *n* a small round piece of hard plastic containing music or other data

cell phone (U.S.) *n* a mobile or portable telephone

Celsius *n* a unit of temperature measurement

centimeter (U.S.), centimetre (U.K.) *n* a metric unit of length (one-hundredth of a meter)

certificate *n* an official document recording a fact or achievement (such as a birth certificate)

chair *n* a movable seat with a back for one person

chairlift *n* a series of chairs hung from a moving cable, usually used for taking passengers up mountains to ski

change *v* to make different, to alter; to clean and put a new diaper on a baby; to exchange one form of currency for another; *n* a small amount of coins; of the amount of money paid which is more than the value of goods bought and which is normally given back to the person paying

charcoal *n* a black natural substance used for creating heat on a barbecue

charge *v* to ask for an amount of money for goods or services; to give power to an electrical item (such as a mobile phone), usually with a small device

charge *n* the amount of money needed to buy goods or services

cheap *adj* low in price

cheaper *comp adj* less expensive than another item

check *v* to look carefully at something to make sure it is accurate or in good condition; *n* (U.S.) the bill

check account **(U.S.)** *n* a bank (current) account

check in *v* to go to a desk and show that you are ready to stay in a hotel or to board an aircraft; to hand in a piece of luggage for transportation (such as to check in a suitcase for a flight)

check-in *n* the desk at an airport or hotel where a person checks in

check out *v* to leave a hotel

check-out *n* a cash desk at a supermarket

cheers *int* used when you raise a glass of alcohol to wish others good health; (U.K.) thank-you; (U.K.) good-bye

chemical toilet *n* a portable toilet usually used when camping

chemist's (U.K.) *n* a shop that sells medicines and items for personal hygiene

cheque (U.K.) *n* a signed document

used for payment for goods or services (a banker's draft)

chest *n* the front part of the human body from the neck to the stomach

chewing gum *n* a flavored sweet that you chew but do not swallow

child *n* a boy or a girl

child's seat *n* a chair specifically designed for a small boy or girl

children's menu *n* a selection of food options suitable for children

children's portion *n* a small portion of food

chopsticks *n.pl.* two small sticks of wood used to eat with (esp. by Chinese people)

church *n* a place where Christians go to pray

cigar *n* a roll of tobacco leaf for smoking

cigarette *n* cut tobacco rolled in paper for smoking

class *n* a number of students taught together; a category of travel (such as *first and second class* on a train)

classical music *n* traditional music played by an orchestra

clean *v* to make something less dirty; *adj* free from dirt

clear *v* to free from objects; *adj* bright (such as *it is a clear day*), not obstructed

cliff *n* a large rock with a very steep side

cling film® **(U.K.)** *n* a thin plastic film used for wrapping things, usually food

close *v* to shut

closed *adj* not open

close *adv* near to

clothes *n.pl.* to the things that people wear to cover their bodies

clothes store *n* a shop which sells clothes

club *n* a place or site where people who have similar interests meet or the people who meet there; a nightclub

coat *n* a piece of clothing that is worn over other clothes, usually to keep you warm

coffee shop *n* a cafe specialising in hot drinks, especially coffee

coin *n* a (usually round) metal object used as money

colander *n* a bowl with small holes in it that is used to separate food from liquids

cold *n* a sickness that makes you sneeze, cough and find it hard to breathe; *adj* low in temperature

colleague *n* a person somebody works with

cologne *n* a liquid that smells sweet and is put on your wrists or on your face after you shave

comb *n* a piece of plastic or metal with very thin teeth which is used for styling hair

come *v* to arrive or move towards a place

complain *v* to say that you do not like something or are annoyed

complaint *n* a statement that you do not like something or are annoyed

computer *n* an electronic device for storing and processing data, and also for accessing the internet and playing video games

concert *n* a public musical performance or show

concert hall *n* a place where musical entertainment is offered

condition *n* a state of health or fitness; a medical problem

conditioner *n* a lotion used after shampooing to make your hair softer

condom *n* a device worn over the penis during sex to prevent the woman from becoming pregnant or to avoid catching a disease

conference *n* a meeting of business people

confirm *v* to say that something is

definitely true or that something will take place (such as a fact or appointment)

congestion n a situation where there is too much traffic; a feeling in the nose where you find it hard to breathe

connect v to join together; to gain access to the internet via a computer

connection n an additional flight, train or bus ride that forms part of a scheduled journey; a telephone or internet link

constipation n a medical condition whereby a person has difficulty getting rid of solid waste from his or her body

consulate n the offices of the official representative of a foreign country

consultant n an expert who gives advice; a senior doctor

contact v to get in touch with someone

contact lens n a thin piece of plastic worn instead of eyeglasses to help you see better

contact lens solution n a cleaning fluid for contact lenses

contagious adj of a disease which is easily spreadable or infectious

continental breakfast n a breakfast usually consisting of coffee or tea, fruit juice, bread, butter, cheese and jam

convention hall n a building (usually large) in which exhibitions, conferences and events are held

conveyor belt n a mechanical band or moving platform which carries objects (such as groceries in a shop or luggage at an airport)

cook v to prepare food by heating

cooking gas n fuel used for operating an oven or stove

cool adj slightly cold but pleasant

copper n a red-brown metal

corkscrew n a tool for removing corks from bottles

cost n the price charged or paid for a thing

cot n a crib

cotton n a natural fabric used to make clothing

cough v to let out air from the lungs in a sudden and noisy manner; n the act of coughing; a medical condition caused by frequent coughing

country code n the numbers that have to be dialled before a telephone number to make a call to another country

cover charge n the amount added

to a restaurant bill to cover service; the price of entrance into a bar or nightclub

crash v a situation where two or more vehicles hit each other violently

cream n an ointment or lotion applied to the skin; a sweet dairy product (which often accompanies a desert)

credit card n a plastic card issued by a bank or business to allow the user to receive goods or services and pay for them later

crib (U.S.) n a small bed with high sides for a young child

crystal n a clear transparent mineral

cup n a container to drink from

currency n the system of money of a country (such as the U.S. dollar)

currency exchange v the conversion of one currency of money into another

currency exchange office n a place for exchanging currency (bureau de change)

current account n a bank account for putting in and taking out money, usually with low interest

custom n a traditional way of behaving, specific to a country or society

customs n the place at an airport or international entry point where officials check your bags or vehicle for goods which taxes have to be paid on or which are not allowed in the country

cut v to divide something into smaller parts with a knife or something similar; to injure skin or flesh with a knife or something similar; n an injury caused by cutting

cute n attractive in a sweet way

cycle v to ride a bicycle

D

damage v to inflict harm upon something or someone; n physical harm to something that prevents it from working normally

dance v to move your body to the rhythm of music

dance club n a nightclub or disco

dangerous adj likely to cause physical harm or problems

dark adj with little or no light; approaching black in color

date n a day of a month or year; a fixed point of time

day n a 24-hour period between midnight and midnight; the hours when it is not night

deaf n unable to hear

debit card *n* a plastic card issued by a bank to allow the user to use money held in an account to pay for goods or services

deck chair (U.K.) *n* a collapsible chair, camp-stool or long chair for reclining in

declare *v* to make known or to announce to other people

decline *v* to say no to an offer or request

deep *adj* going far down; intense or serious (such as *a deep love of music*)

degree *n* the unit of measurement of temperature; an document which shows you have completed a university course

delay *n* a situation where someone or something has to wait or when something does not happen when it should happen

delay *v* to make someone or something late; to put off till later

delete *v* to remove text or files from a document or computer

delicatessen *n* a shop or counter selling cooked meats, cheeses and the like

delicious *adj* with a very good taste (as in food)

denim *n* a very strong cotton fabric

used in clothing (specifically jeans)

dentist *n* a person qualified in treating people's teeth

dentures *n.pl.* a set of false teeth

deodorant *n* a substance that removes or hides unpleasant smells on the human body

department store *n* a shop selling a great variety of goods

departures *n* the area at an airport for passengers who are about to leave on a flight

deposit *v* to put money into a bank account, or an object into storage; *n* part of the price of goods or a service which is paid in advance; a sum of money paid when renting something like a car which is given back if the car is returned with no damage

desert *n* a region with no trees or water and a lot of sand, usually with very hot temperatures

detergent *n* a liquid or powder for cleaning clothes or surfaces

detour *n* a different road or path (for instance when there is an accident on the road)

develop *v* (of a camera film) to process an image stored on a camera film into a photograph

diabetes *n* a disease in which you have too much sugar in your blood

diabetic *n* a person suffering from diabetes

dial *v* to enter a number into a telephone to make a call

diamond *n* a valuable, clear precious stone

diaper *n* (U.S.) a type of underwear for babies that holds liquid and solid waste from the baby and is usually thrown away after use

diarrhea (U.S.), diarrhoea (U.K.) *n* an illness where waste from the body is soft and comes out often

diesel *n* a heavy fuel oil used to power diesel engines in vehicles

difficult *adj* hard to do or carry out

digital *adj* relating to computer technology

digital camera *n* a camera that records and stores images in electronic form

digital photo *n* an image made by a digital camera, which can be displayed on a screen or electronic device

dining room *n* a room in a house or building for eating meals in

dinner *n* the main meal of the day

direction *n* the way towards which

something is traveling

directions *n.pl.* instructions on how to get to a place or do something

dirty *adj* not clean or washed

disabled *adj* having a condition in which part of your mind or body does not function

disconnect *v* to remove one thing from another (such as an item of hardware from a computer); to log off the internet

discount *n* a reduction of the price of goods or services

dish *n* a broad, shallow, open container for cooking or serving up food

dishwasher *n* a machine for washing dishes, pots, pans, knives, forks

dishwashing liquid *n* a liquid used for washing dishes

display *v* to put out for people to see;

display case *n* a container with a glass front where objects (often expensive ones) are shown

disposable *n* any item intended for throwing away after use

disposable razor *n* a razor that can be thrown away after use

dive *v* to plunge head first under water; to swim underwater using a special device for breathing

diving equipment *n* the equipment

needed to go dive under water

divorce *n* the legal ending of a marriage

divorce *v* to end a marriage legally

dizzy *adj* feeling unable to stand straight (for instance after spinning round or when you look down from a high place)

doctor *n* a person qualified to treat people who are ill

doll *n* a child's toy which looks like a human figure (often female)

dollar *n* the unit of currency in the U.S., Canada, Australia, New Zealand and other countries

domestic *adj* relating to the home or household, or the internal aspect of a country

domestic flight *n* an airplane journey within the country where you take off

door *n* an entrance and exit that can be opened and closed

dormitory *n* a large room for sleeping that contains a number of beds (such as in a hostel)

double bed *n* a wide bed for two people

downtown *n* the business and commercial center of a city. *adv* moving towards the center

dozen *n* 12 items

dress *n* an item of clothing (usually for females) that covers the top of the body and part of the legs

dress code *n* the type of clothing required for a restaurant, party etc

drink *v* to swallow a liquid; *n* a liquid to be drunk

drinks menu *n* a list of drinks available in a bar or restaurant

drinking water *n* water suitable for drinking

drive *v* to control a vehicle

driver's license (U.S.), driving licence (U.K.) *n* document stating that a person is qualified to drive a vehicle

drop *n* a very small quantity of liquid

drowsy *adj* sleepy

dry clean *v* to clean clothes using chemicals instead of water

dry cleaner *n* a place or business cleans clothes with chemicals

dub *v* to give a new sound-track (usually in a different language) to a film

during *prep.* over a certain period of time of or while something is happening

duty *n* a tax that has to be paid on goods or a service

duty-free *adj* free from tax (often

applied to goods purchased at an airport)

DVD *n* a disc for playing and recording films, images or data

E

ear *n* the organ of hearing

earache *n* a pain in the ears

early *adj* coming or happening before or in advance of the usual time; situated in or near the beginning

earrings *n* jewellery worn on the ears

east *n* the direction opposite to west; the point of the compass where the sun rises

easy *adj* not difficult to do

eat *v* to put food into your mouth and swallow it

economy class *n* the cheapest or most basic section of seating and service on an airplane or other form of transport

elbow *n* the joint between the lower and upper arm

elevator (U.S.) *n* a machine that takes people from floor to floor

email *v* to send an electronic message

email address *n* the name of a person's e-mail account

emergency *n* a sudden serious occurrence or situation that requires immediate action

emergency exit *n* a door for exiting a building or vehicle in case of fire or other serious incident

empty *v* to remove the contents from something

enamel *n* hard substance like milky glass that is used for decorative purposes

end *v* to bring or come to a finish

English *adj* relating to a person or thing from England; *n* the language of the British Isles, North America, Australasia, parts of Southern Africa, and other parts of the British Commonwealth

engrave *v* to cut letters into an item (such as a piece of jewellery)

enjoy *v* to take pleasure in something

enter *v* to go or come into a place

entertainment *n* an activity or event that provides pleasure or amusement to people

entrance *n* the way into a building or place

envelope *n* a paper cover to contain a letter

equipment *n* things needed for carrying out a particular activity

escalator *n* a moving staircase

e-ticket *n* a ticket for travel printed off from a computer

EU resident *n* a citizen of country belonging to the European Union

euro *n* the single currency of a large number of member states of the European Union

evening *n* the period from the end of the (working) day till you go to bed

excess *n* an amount of something that is more than necessary

excess luggage *n* an item or items of luggage that go over the weight limits set by an airline and which have to be paid for

exchange *v* to give or receive in return for something else; to change money into another currency; *n* a place or business for exchanging currency

exchange rate *n* the price which has to be paid in one currency for an amount in the currency of another country

excursion *n* a journey or trip made for pleasure (usually short and organised)

excuse me *int* a polite phrase used when you want to ask someone something; (U.S.) a polite phrase used when you want someone to say something again

exhausted *adj* extremely tired or with no energy

exit *v* to leave or go out of a place; *n* the way out of a place or building

expensive *adj* high in price; the opposite of cheap

expert *n* a person who has special skills or knowledge

express *adv* done with speed; *n* a fast, direct service (such as a bus or train)

extension *n* the numbers required to reach one telephone in a system with many lines

extra *adj* beyond what is absolutely necessary; larger or better than is usual; n an additional object or service

extra large *n (of clothing)* a size that is very large

extract *v* to pull out *(of a tooth)*

eye *n* one of the organs on the face used for seeing

F

face *n* the front part of the head

facial *n* a beauty treatment for the face

family *n* people that are related to one another

fan *n* a piece of equipment used for cooling purposes

far *adj* at or to a long distance from

farm *n* an area of land used under one management where crops are grown or livestock such as cows are kept

far-sighted *adj* unable to see close objects clearly

fast *adj* quick, speedy

fast food *n* food which can be prepared and served very quickly (such as burgers)

fat free *adj* not containing animal or vegetable fats

father *n* a male parent

fax *n* a system for sending documents electronically; *v* to send a fax

feed *v* to give food to

ferry *n* a large boat for transporting passengers and vehicles across a body of water

fever *n* an illness in which you have a high body temperature and usually a headache

field *n* an area where sports are played; a piece of farmland

fill *v* to put or pour into until no more can be admitted; fill in *or* out *v* to enter details in a form

filling *n* material used to fill up a hole in a tooth

film *n* a story shown in words and moving pictures in a cinema or on TV; a thin piece of plastic used for capturing images in a camera

fine *n* money that has to be paid for breaking a law

finger *n* one of the four digits (as distinguished from the thumb) on a hand

fingernail *n* the hard part on the front of the finger tip

fire *n* combustion or burning that gives off extreme heat and smoke

fire department (U.S.), fire brigade (U.K.) *n* the emergency service responsible for putting out fires

firedoor a door designed to prevent the spread of fire

first *adj* coming before any other in order, time, place, rank, importance or excellence;

first-class *n* a section of seating and service (such as on an airplane or other form of transport) that is superior to all other classes

fitting room *n* a private area in a shop where customers can try on clothes

fix *v* to repair or mend

flashlight (U.S.) *n* a device that you carry in your hand and that has an electric light

flat tire (U.S.), flat tyre (U.K.) a tire with very little or no air in it

flight *n* a journey on an aircraft

floor *n* the bottom surface of a room; a level in a building (such as a hotel

flower *n* the part of a plant which has seeds, often smells pleasantly and is often colorful and attractive to look at

folk music *n* the traditional popular music of a people or culture

food *n* things that are eaten by humans or animals

foot *n* the part of the body which you walk on

football *n (U.S.)*; a game between two teams in which a football is handled and kicked, to score goals or points; (U.K.) soccer; the ball used in such a game

for *prep* in support or favour of; with regard to; having as a purpose

forecast *v* to say something will happen in the future; *n* a statement of what the weather is going to be like

forest *n* an area of trees

fork *n* a tool with which you pick up food and which has several long points

form *n* a document with blank spaces for information to be filled in

formula *n* special milk for feeding to babies

fountain *n* a structure in which water is pushed into the air, usually for decoration

free *adj* (goods or service) available for no charge

freezer *n* a device which keeps food at temperatures below zero(often for long periods)

French *adj* relating to a person or thing from France; *n* the language of the people of France

fresh *adj* (of fruit, flowers, etc) picked, prepared, or cut a short time ago

friend *n* a person you know well and like

frying pan *n* a shallow metal pan with a long handle, in which food is fried

full-time *adv* for the whole of the (standard) working week

G

game *n* an activity in which people play against each other as a sport or for entertainment (such as a *board game* or *computer game*)

garage *n* a building in which a car or cars are kept; (U.K.) a place which sells fuel for cars and other vehicles

garbage bag *n* a plastic bag for things you want to throw away

gas *n* a fuel for lighting and heating; (U.S.) a fuel for powering vehicles

gas station (U.S.) *n* a place which sells fuel for cars and other vehicles

gate *n* the place at an airport where you board an aircraft

gay *n* a homosexual person

gay bar *n* a bar popular with homosexual men or women

gel *n* a thick substance for styling hair

get off *v* to get out of a vehicle

get to *v* to reach or arrive at

gift *n* something you give to someone, often on a special occasion such as a birthday

gift shop *n* a shop selling souvenirs or items suitable as gifts

girl *n* a female child

girlfriend *n* a female partner with whom a man or woman has a romantic or sexual relationship

give *v* to pass something on to someone else

glass *n* the material used to make windows and which you can see through; a container made of this material which you can drink from

glasses *n* a pair of lenses in a frame that perch on the nose to aid a person's vision

go *v* to move from one place to another; to leave

gold *n* a precious metal of a bright yellow color

golf course *n* an area of land on which golf is played

golf tournament *n* an organised golf competition

good afternoon *int* a formal greeting used when you meet or leave someone in the afternoon

good evening *int* a formal greeting used when you meet or leave someone in the evening

good morning *int* a formal greeting used when you meet or leave someone in the morning

good-bye *int* an expression used when you meet or leave someone

goods *n* things that are made for selling

gram (U.S.), gramme (U.K.) *n* a standard unit of weight in the metric system; there are 1000 grams in a kilogram

grandchild *n* the child of a person's son or daughter

grandfather *n* the father of a person's parent

grandmother *n* the mother of a person's parent

grandparent *n* the mother or father of a person's parent

gray (U.S.), grey (U.K.) *adj* of a color between white and black; the color of the sky when there is a lot of cloud

green *adj* of the color of grass

grocery store *n* a food shop

ground floor (U.K.) *n* the part of a building level with the ground outside (in America called the first floor)

groundcloth (U.S.) *n* a piece of material which water cannot get through and which is spread on the floor to protect against dampness (such as inside or beneath a tent)

groundsheet (U.K.) *n* a groundcloth

group *n* people who are together in one place (often to take part in the same activity); people who have the same interests

guide *n* a person with special knowledge of an area who leads a party of tourists

guidebook *n* a book for tourists, describing places of interest and practical information

guide-dog *n* a dog trained to lead a blind person

gym *n* a building or room where athletic exercises are performed (short for gymnasium)

gynecologist (U.S.), gynaecologist (U.K.) *n* a doctor who specializes in the functions and diseases peculiar to women

H

hair *n* the strands that grow on the head and other parts of the body

hairdrier, hairdryer *n* an electric device for drying the hair by blowing hot air

hairbrush *n* a brush for styling the hair

haircut *n* the act or style of cutting someone's hair

hair-salon *n* a place where hair is cut and styled

hair-spray *n* a sticky liquid for the hair sprayed from an aerosol can

hairstyle *n* a particular way of arranging the hair

hair-stylist *n* a skilled person who cuts and styles hair

half *n* one of two equal parts into which a thing is or may be divided

half-hour *n* 30 minutes

half-kilo *n* 500 grams

hammer *n* a tool for hitting nails into wood

hand *n* the end part of the arm beyond the wrist

hand luggage *n* item or items of luggage permitted to be taken into the cabin of an aircraft

handbag (U.K.) *n* a small bag for carrying things (usually for females)

handicapped *adj* having a condition in which part of your mind or body does not function

hangover *n* the unpleasant feeling the day after drinking too much alcohol

happy *adj* feeling or showing pleasure

hat *n* an item of clothing worn on the head

head *n* the top part of the human body above the neck

headache *n* a pain in the head

headphones *n* a device that fits on or in the ears, for privately listening to music or sound

health *n* a measure or state of wellness

health-food store *n* a shop selling nutritious or organic food products

heart *n* the body's central organ of blood circulation

heart-condition *n* having a weak or medically damaged heart

heat *n* a form of energy that provides warmth

heater *n* a device that gives off warmth

hectare *n* a measure of area equal to 100,000 square metres or 2.471 acres

hello *int* an informal or friendly greeting

helmet *n* a hard hat that protects the head

help *v* to give aid or assistance to (a cause or person); *n* aid or assistance

here *n* in or at this place, point or time

hi *int.* an informal or friendly greeting

high *adj* situated far from the ground

high chair *n* a baby's chair with long legs and a tray so the baby can sit at a table

high-heeled shoes *n* a pair of shoes with a tall heel (usually for females)

highway *n* a main road route

hiking boots *n* strong shoes specifically designed for walking on rough terrain

hill *n* a natural piece of land that is higher than the area around it; a small mountain

hire *v* to pay for the use of something, usually for a short period

hire car *n* a car you pay for to use, usually for a short period

hitch-hike *v* to travel by getting free rides from passing motorists

hockey *n* (U.S.) a game played on ice by teams of skaters with sticks and a small, round flat piece of rubber which they try to score goals with; (U.K.) a team sport involving hitting a ball with a stick with a curved end

holiday *n* a day or longer off work; a

day when people do not have to go to work or school (usually a special day on which something is remembered); (U.K.) a vacation

horsetrack *n* a place where horses race and people bet on which one will win

hospital *n* a place where the sick or injured receive medical treatment

hostel *n* a place providing cheap accommodation, usually for young people

hot *adj* having a high temperature; spicy (food)

hot spring a spring of naturally hot water

hotel *n* a business place providing accommodation and meals for travellers

hour *n* 60 minutes

house *n* a building where people live

household goods *n* items for use in the home

housekeeping service *n* cleaning a hotel room or house

how *adv* in what way or manner; by what means; to what extent

how much? used to ask what the price of something is

hug *v* to put your arms around someone and hold him or her close

hungry *adj* a feeling the need to eat something; having a keen appetite

hurt *v* to cause physical or emotional pain

husband *n* the person a woman is married to

I

ibuprofen *n* a drug which reduces pain and fever

ice *n* frozen water

ice hockey (U.K.) *n* see hockey

icy *adj* a surface covered in ice, usually slippery or dangerous to walk or travel on

identification *n* an official proof of identity, such as a driving licence, passport or ID card

ill *adj* not in good health

image *n* a representation of someone or something as taken by a camera

include *v* to have as part of a something (as in included in the price = with no extra costs)

indoor pool *n* a swimming pool which is inside a building

inexpensive *adj* cheap, not costing a lot

infected *adj* containing bacteria

information *n* the act of providing facts or details about something

information desk *n* a kiosk or office

providing information to visitors to a place

insect *n* a small creature with six legs and usually with wings (such as a fly or wasp)

insect bite *n* a sting, wound or bite caused by an insect

insect repellent *n* a spray or lotion applied to the skin to prevent insect bites

insert *v* to place one object within another (such as *to insert a card into a machine*)

insomnia *n* the inability to sleep or sleep well

instant message *n* a message sent via the internet that appears straight away to the person you are contacting

insurance *n* an agreement with a company in which you pay them a sum of money (regularly) and they pay you if have an accident, are injured, something is stolen, damaged or something similar happens

insurance company *n* a business which offers insurance services

interesting *adj* arousing attention or curiosity

international *adj* relating to different countries; the area at an airport where flights depart to and arrive from other countries

international flight *n* an aircraft journey that crosses into another country

international student card *n* a card that shows you are a student, which means you can get discounts and other privileges

internet *n* a global computer network

internet cafe *n* a place that allows paying customers to use computers to access the internet

interpreter *n* a person who translates what someone says into another language

intersection *n* a junction or crossroads on a main road

intestine *n* the part of a person's body where food is broken down

introduce *v* to cause a person to meet a new person

invoice *n* a document showing the cost of a service or goods

Irish *adj* relating to a person or thing from Ireland

iron *n* a household device for making clothes smooth; *v* to smooth clothes with this device

Italian *adj* relating to a person or thing

from Italy

itemized check (U.S.), itemized bill (U.K.) *n* a receipt showing the price of each individual item

J

jacket *n* a piece of clothing that is like a short coat

jar *n* a container (often made from glass) used to keep objects or food products in

jaw *n* one of two bones in the mouth which hold the teeth in place

jazz *n* a type of music of black American origin, with a strong emphasis on rhythm and in which the musicians often play pieces on their own

jazz club *n* a place where live jazz is played

jeans *n* pants (U.K.: trousers) made from a strong material called denim

Jet Ski® *n* a small, powerful water vehicle on which one or two people can travel over the water for pleasure

jeweler (U.S.), jeweller (U.K.) *n* a maker of or dealer in necklaces, rings, bracelets, and other fashion items

jewelry (U.S.), jewellery (U.K.) *n* personal items (such as necklaces, rings, or bracelets) often containing precious stones or made from precious metal

join *v* to sit or stand together with someone

joint *n* a part in the body where two bones come together

journey *n* the act of traveling to a place

K

key *n* a (usually) metal instrument for opening or closing locks

key card *n* a plastic card that opens electronic locks (often in hotels)

key ring *n* a ring for carrying keys

kiddie pool *n* a shallow swimming pool for children

kidney *n* one of the body's vital organs

kilogram, also kilogramme (U.K.) *n* a measure of weight (1,000 grams or 2.2046 pounds)

kilometer (U.S.), kilometre (U.K.) *n* a measure of distance (1,000 meters or 0.621 mile)

kiss *v* to touch someone with your lips as a greeting or to show your love

kitchen *n* the room in a house or building where food is cooked or prepared

kitchen foil *n* aluminum foil used for wrapping food to keep it fresh

knee *n* the joint between the upper

and lower parts of the leg

knife *n* an implement for cutting, consisting of blade and handle

L

lace *n* a decorative fabric; a cord or string used to tie shoes

lactose intolerant *adj* unable to digest lactose, a sugar derived from milk found in milk and other dairy products

lake *n* a large body of water entirely surrounded by land

large *adj* great, big or bulky in size; *n* the clothing or product size that is bigger than medium

last *adj* coming after all others or at the end

late *adj* coming after the proper or usual time; far on in a period of time

Laundromat® *n* a place where people can use washing-machines which require coins to operate

laundry *n* a place where clothes are washed and ironed; the clothes sent to or received from a laundry

law *n* the rules that people in a country must obey

lawyer *n* a professional legal expert

leather *n* a material made from the specially treated skin of an animal

(usually used in clothing and on furniture)

leave *v* to go away from a place; to place something somewhere for storage (as in leave your bags at the station); not to move, change, remove or interfere with something

left *adj* on or to the side of your body that contains your heart

leg *n* one of the limbs on which humans and other mammals walk or stand

legal *adj* having to do with the law

lens *n* a piece of curved glass or other transparent material (such as in a camera or pair of contact lenses)

less *n* a smaller amount of something; *adv* smaller in quantity, extent, number or importance

lesson *n* a period of instruction or learning in a particular subject

letter *n* a written message sent to another person; a character in writing which represents a spoken sound

library *n* a building with a collection of books which people can borrow

life jacket *n* a piece of clothing that can be filled with to keep a person afloat in water

lifeguard *n* a person at a beach or pool who gives aid to swimmers in difficulties

lift (U.K.) *n* an elevator; a (usually short) trip together in someone else's vehicle

lift pass *n* a ticket enabling people to use the chair-lifts on a ski slope

light *v* to cause something (such as a cigarette) to burn; *adj* bright, clear, not dark; not heavy in weight

light-bulb *n* a glass object in a lamp which glows when an electric current is passed through it

lighter *n* a device for lighting cigarettes

like *v* to be pleased with; to be attracted by; to enjoy or to be fond of

line *n* a track or route used by a train

linen *n* sheets used to cover a bed

lip *n* one of the two fleshy parts around the opening of the mouth

liquor store (U.S.) *n* a shop that sells alcoholic drinks

liter (U.S.), litre (U.K.) *n* a unit of capacity in the metric system, equal to around 1.75 pints

little *adv* in a small degree; *n* not much (as in a little); *adj* small, not great or big in size

live *v* to be alive; to have your home in a certain place

live adj performing in front of an audience (as in live music)

liver *n* a vital organ that purifies the blood

Loafer® *n.pl.* a low leather shoe that slips onto the foot

local *adj* belonging or relating to a particular area or place

lock *n* a device for securing doors or other objects so that they cannot be opened; *v* to secure a door or other objects so that they cannot be opened

locker *n* a cupboard or chest that can be locked and where you can leave things in public places

log off *v* to end or sign out of a computer or online session

log on *v* to begin or sign into a computer or online session

long *adj* of considerable length; measuring a great distance; covering a great period of time

long-sighted *adj* able to see to a great distance; unable to see close things clearly

look *v* to direct the eye towards something in order to see it; to search for something

lose *v* to stop having something, often suddenly; to be unable to find something; to fail to win

lost *adj* unable to find the way; no longer held or had by someone

lotion *n* a liquid that is put on the skin to make it soft or to protect it

loud *adj* powerful in sound; noisy

love *n* a feeling of deep fondness, affection and devotion towards a person or thing; *v* to have strong affection for, to be fond of, to have strong romantic feelings for someone

low *adj* not reaching a great height or level; below a particular marker or level

luggage *n* the cases and other things a traveller has on a journey

luggage cart *n* a flat vehicle for placing and transporting luggage (such as in a hotel or at an airport)

lunch *n* the meal usually eaten in the middle of the day

lung *n* one of the two organs of the body with which you breathe

M

magazine *n* a publication that appears usually once every week or month and contains articles by different people on various topics

magnificent *adj* very beautiful

mail *n* letters or parcels delivered by post; an email message

mail box (U.S.) *n* a public box into which mail is placed for collection and delivery; a private box on a person's property for receiving post

main attraction *n* a principal or popular tourist spot in a location

main course *n* the principal serving or dish in a meal (usually savoury)

mall *n* an indoor shopping center

man *n* a male adult

manager *n* a person in charge of running a business, establishment or team of people

manicure *n* a treatment of the hands and fingernails to make them look better

manual car *n* a car in which the driver has to change gears (as opposed to an automatic car)

map *n* a drawing of an area of land or sea showing its most important features; a printed diagram of a system (such as the subway) or showing how to get to a particular place

market *n* a place where people buy and sell goods (such as food or crafts), usually outside, from stands

marry *v* to become man and wife

married *adj* having a husband or wife

mass *n* a church service, especially in

the Roman Catholic church

massage *n* a treatment in which someone rubs the muscles in your body with their hands

match *n* a sporting contest; a small wooden strip for lighting a fire

meal *n* food taken at a particular set time of day (such as breakfast, lunch or dinner)

measure *v* to find out how big or long something is or how many of something there are

measuring cup *n* a container for measuring the quantity usually of a liquid (mainly used in cooking)

mechanic *n* a person skilled in repairing vehicles

medicine *n* a liquid or tablet for the relief or cure of illness

medium *n* a clothing size between small and large; *adj* average in size

meet *v* to come face to face with or join up with someone

meeting *n* an official coming together (often in business);

meeting room *n* a room (often in a hotel or office) for holding meetings

membership card *n* a card confirming that you are part of an organization or a group

memorial *n* a statue, stone with writing on it or something similar that serves to remember a person or past event

memory card *n* a card for storing data from a computer or images in a digital camera

mend *v* to take measures to make something that is not working work again, or to put right something that is wrong with someone's clothing

menstrual cramp *n* pain experienced by a woman in the time of the month when blood flows from her body

menu *n* the selection of dishes available to order in a restaurant or cafe

message *n* a piece of information, spoken or written, passed on from one person to another

meter[1] **(U.S.), metre (U.K.)** *n* the standard measure of length in the metric system (equivalent to 100 centimeters)

meter[2] *n* a device that indicates how long a person has paid to park a car for; an device which shows how much gas, water, or electricity has been used

microwave *n* an device that uses very short electric waves to heat food very quickly

midday *n* noon; 12pm

midnight *n* 12am or 0:00 hours

mileage *n* the distance or number of miles traveled by a vehicle

mini-bar *n* a refrigerator in a hotel room containing drinks that can be bought

minute *n* a measure of time equal to 60 seconds or one 60th of an hour

missing *adj* not in the place he, she or it should be

mistake *n* something done, written or said the wrong way

mobile home *n* a caravan or house trailer (often situated in a permanent location such as a holiday park)

mobile phone (U.K.) *n* a portable telephone

mobility *n* the ability to move easily

money *n* coins or notes of a particular currency

month *n* one of the twelve parts into which the year is divided

mop *n* a tool with a long handle and thick strings for cleaning floors

moped *n* a vehicle with two wheels and a small motor

more *n a* greater amount; *adv* greater in quantity, extent, number or importance

morning *n* the first part of the day, from dawn to midday

mosque *n* a place where Muslims go to pray

mother *n* a female parent

motion sickness *n* nausea felt when traveling in a car, ship or aircraft

motor boat *n* a boat with a motor

motorcycle *n* a vehicle with two wheels and a motor (which is sometimes very powerful)

motorway (U.K.) *n* a highway for fast motor traffic, usually with many lanes and high speed limits

mountain *n* a very big, steep hill rising high above the surrounding land

mousse *n* a dessert made from cream, eggs, and fruit or chocolate

mouth *n* the opening in the face for eating, drinking, breathing and speaking

movie *n* a story shown in words and moving pictures in a cinema or on TV

movie theater *n* a building for showing movies (a cinema)

mug *v* to rob someone using or threatening to use violence

muscle *n* the tissue in your body that enables you to move

museum *n* a room or building where objects of interest or importance are shown to the public

music *n* the art of making a series of sounds which are pleasing to the ear through song and/or instruments

N

nail file *n* a device for smoothing and shaping fingernails

nail salon *n* a place for the treatment of fingernails and manicures

name *n* a word or words by which a person or place is known or identified

napkin *n* a small cloth or piece of paper used to protect clothes while eating

nappy (U.K.) *n* a diaper

nationality *n* the status of belonging to or coming from a particular country

nature preserve *n* a designated, protected area of land, usually containing a natural feature of beauty

nausea *n* a feeling of sickness

near *adv* at or to a short distance from; close to in place or time

nearby *adv* only a short distance from a particular place

near-sighted *adj* unable to see clearly at a distance

neck *n* the narrow portion of the body connecting the head to the shoulders

necklace *n* a string of beads or gems worn round the neck

necktie *n* (U.S.) a strip of material worn and knotted around the neck of a shirt, usually by men

need *v* to have to have something (usually in order to do something)

newspaper *n* a printed publication containing news, opinions and special features (usually published daily or weekly)

newsstand *n* a street kiosk selling newspapers and magazines

next *adj* immediately following; nearest in place, time or degree

nice *adj* pleasant, attractive, friendly

night *adj* the time of darkness from sunset to sunrise

nightclub *n* a place which sells alcohol, offers entertainment, and is open late at night

no *adv* a word used to answer a question negatively (opposite of yes); not one, not any (as in no towels)

non-alcoholic *adj* (of a drink) not containing alcohol

non-smoking *adj* (of a place) where smoking is not allowed

noon *n* the middle of the day, 12:00pm

north *n* one of the 4 points on the compass, the direction towards the top of the globe, opposite to south

nose *n* the part of the middle of the face used for breathing and smelling

note *n* a written message or memo; a piece of paper used as money; *v* to pay special attemtion to

nothing *pron* not anything; no thing that exists

notify *v* to make known or to inform

novice *n* a beginner, a person with little experience at something

now *adv* at the present time

number *n* a word or sign (such as nine and 9) that represents a certain quantity of something; a short form of phone number

nurse *n* a person who tends to people who are sick or injured

O

office *n* a place of work or business (either a room or building);

office hours *n* the times of day that a place is open for business (often 9:00am to 5:00pm)

off-licence (U.K.) *n* a shop that sells alcohol

oil *n* a liquid fuel derived from petroleum; a natural liquid used in cooking

OK *adv* used in spoken language to show you agree with something

old *adj* having existed for many years

once *adv* one time; one time only; at some point in the past

one the number 1; *pron* a single thing

one-way (U.S.) *adj* a ticket for travel to a place but not back again

one-way street *n* a street where travel in only one direction is allowed

only *adj* solitary, single or alone in its kind; *adv* no more than

open *v* (of doors, etc) to make something so that it can be moved through; (of store etc) to start business for the day; *adj* not closed or blocked; (of store etc) doing business

opera *n* a dramatic performance in which the dialog is sung to music

opera house *n* a theater where operas are performed

opposite *adj* on the other side of something or facing something

optician *n* a person who tests someone's eyes and can provide her or him with eyeglasses or contact lenses

orange *adj* of the color when red and yellow are mixed; *n* a round fruit of this color

orchestra *n* a group of musicians who play many different instruments and usually play classical music

order v to ask for something to eat or drink in a restaurant; to tell someone what to do

outdoor pool n a swimming pool located outside

outside adv not in a building

over-the-counter adj (of medication) available without a prescription

overlook (U.S.) n a high place from which an attraction can be seen

overnight adv in the course of the night or evening

P

pacifier (AE) n a rubber object which a baby is given for sucking

pack v to put items for travel into a suitcase or bag

package n goods in a box and wrapped up for sending by mail

paediatrician (U.K.) n a doctor who specializes in treating children

pain n the unpleasant feeling you have when your body hurts or something is troubling your mind

pajamas (U.S.) n.pl. soft pants and a top worn for sleeping

palace n a building in which a king or queen lives or lived

panties (U.S.) n underwear worn by women or girls

pants n **(U.S.)** clothing worn to cover the legs from the waist to the ankle; **(U.K.)** underwear worn by men or boys

pantyhose (U.S.) n a very thin piece of clothing worn by women to cover the legs from the waist to the toes

paper n thin sheets of material for writing or printing on

paper towel n a piece of paper for drying your hands which is thrown away after use

paracetamol [acetaminnophen] n a mild drug which reduces pain

park v to leave a vehicle in a particular space (usually for a short time); n a piece of land in a town where people can walk and play games

parking lot (U.S.) n a large area where vehicles can be parked (usually for money)

part n one of the individual things that make up the whole of something

part-time adj working in a job for less than the standard weekly hours

pass through v to drive or travel through a location without stopping

passenger n a person who travels by private or public transport (such as a bus or car), but who is not the driver

passport n an official document

authorizing a person to travel in a foreign country

passport control *n* the area in an airport where passports are inspected before departure or after arrival

password *n* a private word or code used for security purposes or to confirm a person's identity

pastry shop *n* a shop that makes and sells sweet baked goods

path *n* a track on which you can walk

pay *v* to hand over money in exchange for goods or services

payphone *n* a public telephone box, operated by money or phone card

peak *n* the highest point of a hill or mountain

pearl *n* a smooth, white or bluish-grey round object found in an oyster shell and used for jewelry

pedestrian *n* a person who travels on foot

pediatrician (U.S.) *n* a doctor who specializes in treating children

pedicure *n* a treatment of feet to make them look better

pen *n* an implement for writing with ink

penicillin *n* a drug used to treat infections caused by bacteria

penis *n* the organ of the male which is used for sex and for passing urine

per *prep* for each (such as *the hotel charges $100 per night*)

perfume *n* a liquid which smells nice and is used to make the body smell nice

period *n* a particular portion of time; the monthly menstruation of women

permit *v* to allow

personal identification number (PIN) *n* a private code with numbers needed to complete a transaction

petite *adj* short, thin and pretty (usually of a woman)

petrol (U.K.) *n* a fuel used to power vehicles

petrol station (U.K.) *n* a place which sells fuel for cars and other vehicles

pewter *n* a material made by mixing tin and lead and used for kitchen utensils

pharmacy *n* a shop that sells medicines

phone *v* to call someone using a telephone; *n* a telephone

phone call *n* a conversation on the telephone

phone card *n* a plastic card loaded with credit for paying for telephone calls

phone number *n* a number required

to contact a person, business or service

photocopy n a copy of a document made by a machine

photograph n an image created using a camera

photography n the process or art of taking images using a camera

pick up v to get something or someone at a particular place and take them with you

picnic area n an area where people can sit and eat outside

piece n a distinct part of something

Pill n a drug taken regularly by a woman to prevent her from becoming pregnant

pillow n a cloth bag with soft material inside for resting the head on during sleep

pink adj of the color between red and white

piste n a slope prepared for skiing

pizzeria n a restaurant where various types of pizza can be bought

place n an area or location; v to put in a particular position

plane n an airplane

plastic wrap n a plastic covering for keeping food fresh

plate n a flat dish from which food is eaten or served

platform n the area at a railway station next to the track, where passengers get on or off trains

platinum n a precious silvery-white metal, used in jewelry

play v to engage in an activity or game for pleasure; to be shown in a movie theater; n a sory performed by actors in a theater

playground n an area, often outdoors, where children can play on special equipment (such as swings)

playpen n a framework inside which young children can play in safety

please adv a polite expression used in when you ask someone to do something or accept something (as in yes, please)

pleasure n a feeling of enjoyment

plunger n a tool with a rubber suction cup on a handle which is used to unblock drains

plus size adj a size of clothing larger than the normal range

pocket n the part of your clothing where you can keep keys, money etc

poison n a substance that injures or kills when you eat or drink it

poles n.pl. long sticks used by skiers to help their balance

police *n.pl.* the group of people whose job it is to keep order, detect crime, and catch criminals

police report *n* an official statement written by the police about a crime or incident

police station *n* the offices of a local section of the police

pond *n* an area of still water, smaller than a lake (often made by humans)

pool *n* a structure filled with water for swimming in

pop music *n* modern music which is popular especially with young people

portable adj capable of being moved easily

portion *n* a part or share of something; an amount of food that is for one person

post *n* the system of delivering letters; an individual letter or item of mail

post-office *n* a place where you can send letters and parcels any buy stamps

post-box (U.K.) *n* a public box into which mail is placed for collection and delivery;

postcard *n* a card with a picture on the front for sending a message from trip

pot *n* a container used for cooking, usually made of metal

pottery *n* dishes, vases and other items made out of baked clay

pound *n* the basic money unit of the U.K., divided into 100 pence

pregnant *adj* (of a woman) with an unborn child inside the body

prescribe *v* to write directions for medical treatment

prescription *n* a piece of paper from the doctor giving the pharmacist instructions about medication for a patient

press *v* to make clothes smooth by applying pressure (such as an iron)

price *n* the amount or price something costs or is being sold for

print *v* to publish or reproduce a page, document, photograph or publication

problem *n* a matter, situation or person that is difficult to deal with or understand

produce *v* to make or create something; to show or provide something

produce store *n* a shop where groceries are sold

prohibit *v* to declare that something must not be done

pronounce *v* to make the correct sound of a word

public *adj* open to the use or

enjoyment of everyone; *n* the people in general

pull *v* to draw or move something towards yourself

purple *adj* of the color created when red and blue are mixed

purse *n* (U.S.) a small bag where a woman keeps her personal items; (U.K.) a very small bag where a woman keeps her money

push *v* to press against something with force to move it

pushchair (U.K.) *n* a light, folding chair on wheels for a child

pyjamas (U.K.) *n.pl.* soft trousers and a top worn for sleeping

Q

qualified *adj* having trained and passed tests in a special field of knowledge

quality *n* degree to which something is good

question *n* a sentence requiring an answer

quiet *adj* low in volume or silent; peaceful or calm

R

racetrack *n* a course around which races take place (athletes, horses, greyhounds or motor vehicles)

racket *n* an instrument made of metal or wood with tight strings in the center for playing sports such as tennis

railway station *n* a place for getting on and off passenger trains

rain *n* the weather condition where moisture falls from the sky

raincoat *n* a waterproof coat for wearing in wet weather

rainforest *n* a dense tropical forest with a very heavy rainfall

rap *n* a form of popular music where the text is spoken to instruments in the background

rape *v* to force (a woman) to have sexual intercourse against her will; *n* sexual intercourse against a person's will

rash *n* an area of spots or patches on the skin

razor *n* a very sharp implement for shaving

razor blade *n* a thin piece of metal with a very sharp edge used in a razor for shaving

reach *v* to extend towards something to touch or hold; to speak to someone on the phone; to arrive at a destination

ready *adj* prepared to do something immediately; fit for immediate use

real *adj* actually existing; not false or fake

receipt *n* a piece of paper confirming the purchase of goods or services

receive *v* to obtain or be given something

reception *n* the entrance area in a hotel where guests check in and out; the celebration after the formal part of a wedding ceremony; the quality of a transmission signal (such as to a mobile phone)

recharge *v* to connect to a power point (such as *to recharge a mobile phone*)

recommend *v* to advise or suggest something as a choice or selection

recycling *n* items of waste that are collected to be used again or made into other products (to help the environment)

red *adj* of a bright warm color, such as blood

refrigerator *n* an electrical kitchen unit for keeping food cold and fresh

region *n* a particular part of a country (usually with its own characteristics)

registered mail *n* a special postal service where the progress of the delivery is followed to ensure that it gets to its destination safely

regular *adj* happening frequently, usually with the same period of time in between; (U.S.) without anything special (as in regular water); *n* a person who goes somewhere on many occasions (such as in *a regular at the bar*); an average sized portion of something (such as a coffee or meal)

relationship *n* a connection to another person by blood, romance, friendship or other common link; a sexual affair

rent *v* to to pay for the use of something, usually for a short period

rental car *n* a vehicle hired for use for a limited time

repair *v* to fix or mend something

repeat *v* to do, make or say over again

reservation *n* an arrangement where a seat, table or room is kept for a particular person (such as in *a dinner reservation*)

reservation desk *n* a desk in a hotel or the like where bookings can be made

reserve *v* to arrange for a seat, table or room to be kept for a particular person

restaurant *n* a place where you can buy and eat a meal at a table

restroom (U.S.) *n* a room with toilet facilities in a public building

retired *adj* having ended an occupation or career because of one's age

return *v* to give something back; *n* (U.K.) a travel ticket for two journeys (to a destination then back again)

rib *n* one of the bones surrounding the upper body

right *adj* relating to the opposite direction to left; correct or true

right of way the entitlement of a vehicle to go first at a junction

ring *n* an item of jewelry that fits round the finger

river *n* a large natural stream of water flowing in a channel usually into the sea

road map *n* a map representing an area's network of roads

rob *v* to take something from someone using force or violence

romantic *adj* relating to the excitement associated with love or sentiment

room *n* a portion of enclosed space in a building; a place for a guest to stay in a hotel

room service *n* the serving of food and drink to guests in their hotel rooms

round-trip (U.S.) *n* a journey to a place and back again

route *n* the course, way or road(s) traveled or to be traveled

rowboat *n* a boat with no engine that is moved with long thin paddles

rubbish *n* things for throwing away

rubbish bag *n* a plastic bag for things you want to throw away

rugby *n* a team sport in which players are allowed to use their hands in carrying and passing an oval ball, tackling opponents, and scoring points by getting the ball across the opponents' goal line

ruins *n* the remains of a structure, building or city that is of historic interest

S

sad *adj* feeling unhappy (usually when something unpleasant has happened)

safe *adj* free or secure from danger or harm; *n* a box made of steel which can be locked and where money, documents, jewelry, etc. can be kept

sales tax *n* a tax that you have to pay in addition to the cost of something you buy

same *adj* identical or similar in kind,

quality, degree

sandals *n.pl* shoes consisting of a flat bottom part and straps, often worn in warm weather or on the beach

sanitary napkin (U.S.) [pad U.K.] *n* a pad worn by a woman in her underwear during menstruation

saucepan *n* a metal pan or pot for boiling or stewing

sauna *n* a very hot room in which you sit and breathe in steam for health reasons

save *v* to stop something dangerous from happening to someone; to keep for later use (as in money); to store what you have done on a computer

savings *n* the money that a person has kept for later use

scanner *n* a machine linked to a computer for copying paper documents or images into electronic form

scarf *n* a long strip of material worn round the neck or over the head for warmth or for fashion reasons

schedule *v* to arrange for a particular time; *n* a printed list of the times of departure and arrival of trains, buses etc

science *n* the study of the physical, chemical and natural world through systematic experiments and research

scissors *n.pl.* an instrument for cutting paper and other material

sea *n* the body of salt water covering most of the earth's surface

seat *n* a place for sitting on (especially in a vehicle, a theater, etc)

security *n* personal safety; the protection of a premises, building, person or thing

see *v* to perceive with the eye

self-service *n* a system used in a shop or restaurant where customers select and collect the goods for themselves (as opposed to *waiter* or *table service*)

sell *v* to give goods or a service to someone in exchange for money

seminar *n* a class or meeting where information on a particular topic is given

send *v* to cause to go somewhere or to someone

senior citizen *n* a person who is of an age at which he or she could retire

separated *adj* no longer living together as a couple

serious *adj* of great importance; very dangerous

service *n* the action of presenting customers with food and drink in a restaurant, or with goods in a shop;

the action of helping people with something they want or need; a religious ceremony

sexually transmitted disease (STD) *n* a disease transmitted through sexual contact

shampoo *n* a liquid used for washing hair

sharp *adj* having a fine edge or point, usually capable of cutting (such as a knife)

shaving cream *n* a foam or gel applied to the face before shaving with a razor

sheet *n* a thin, flat piece of material (such as *a sheet of paper* or *a bed sheet*)

shirt *n* a piece of clothing worn over the upper body and arms and with buttons on the front

ship *v* to send, take or carry an object or goods

shoe store *n* a shop that sells shoes

shoe *n* an object that you wear on your foot, often made of leather

shop *v* to go to stores for the purpose of buying goods

shopping *n* the act of buying goods from stores; goods purchased from stores

shopping centre (U.K.) *n* an area where many shops are located (often indoors)

shopping mall (U.S.) *n* an indoor shopping center

short *adj* not lengthy in time, duration or distance

short-sighted *adj* unable to see clearly at a distance

shorts *n.pl.* a piece of clothing that covers all or part of the upper legs and is usually worn in warm weather

shoulder *n* the part of the body where the arm joins the upper part of the body

show *v* to cause or allow to be seen; to demonstrate

shower *n* bathroom equipment that provides a spray of water for washing; brief, light rainfall

shrine *n* a place where people go to remember something of religious or cultural importance

sick *adj* ill, unwell

side dish *n* an extra, smaller dish or food to go with a main course

side effect *n* a secondary, usually negative, reaction (such as of a drug)

sightseeing *n* going to look at the attractions or notable features of a place

sightseeing tour *n* an excursion or

guided trip for tourists through the attractions of an area

sign *v* to write your name on something to prove that you agree to it (such as a bill)

silk *n* a fine, soft, glossy material used in clothing

single *adj* not married or not in a romantic relationship; consisting of one only

single bed *n* a bed intended to be used by one person

single room *n* a hotel room containing one bed, for one person only

sink *v* (of a ship) to drop beneath the surface of water; *n* a basin with taps which water can be held in (in a bathroom or kitchen)

sister *n* a female born of the same parents as another daughter or son

sit *v* to rest in a position where the weight is supported by the buttocks rather than standing

size *n* the physical characteristics of an object or person; a standard measurement of clothing, drinks and the like (as in size medium)

ski *n* one of two long narrow boards worn on the feet and used for sliding over snow; *v* to move down a snow-covered slope on two long narrow boards worn on the feet

ski lift *n* equipment for transporting people to the top of slope in order to ski down

skin *n* the outer covering of the body

skirt *n* a piece of clothing which hangs from the waist and is worn by women or girls

sleep *v* to rest your body (usually at night and with your eyes closed)

sleeper car *n* a railway carriage fitted with beds for sleeping in

sleeping bag *n* a bag made of warm material for sleeping in when camping

sleepy *adj* in need of rest; (of a place) quiet, with few people around

slice *n* a broad thin piece cut off something (such as in *a slice of bread*); a portion of something (such as cake)

slippers *n.pl.* a pair of comfortable shoes without laces, used indoors

slow *adj* not quick; moving at a low speed

small *adj* not large (in size, stature, degree, amount, number etc)

smoke *v* to breathe in the fumes from a cigarette, cigar or pipe; to use cigarettes etc regularly

smoking *n* the activity of breathing in

smoke from a cigarette etc; adj where the use of cigarettes etc is allowed

snack bar n a place offering light meals or drinks

sneakers n.pl. casual shoes, usually with a rubber sole

snorkeling equipment n the things used for swimming underwater, including a tube for breathing, a mask and fins for the feet

snowboard n a single, short board used for sliding down snowy slopes; n to slide down a hill on a short board

snowshoe n a long, light frame worn on the feet to prevent you sinking when walking on snow

snowy adj covered with snow

soap n a substance used with water for washing the hands or body

soccer (U.K.) n a game between two teams in which a football is kicked, to score goals; the ball used in such a game

sock n a short covering worn on the feet, beneath the shoes

soother (U.S.) n a rubber object which a baby is given for sucking

sore throat n a painful feeling in the throat, which makes it hard to speak or swallow

sorry adj feeling or showing grief or pity; used to express regret when you have done something to hurt someone

south n one of the 4 points on the compass, the direction opposite to north

souvenir n an object bought to remind you of a place you have visited

souvenir store n a shop selling souvenirs and gifts

spa n a place usually with special water, providing relaxation and beauty treatments

spatula n a broad tool used for spreading things (in cooking or decorating)

speak v to talk; to say words

special adj of particular importance; n a dish in a restaurant that is not on the regular menu

specialist n a doctor or surgeon skilled in a particular area of medicine

specimen n a sample of blood or urine taken for medical analysis

speed n the rate someone or something moves at; quick movement; v to travel faster than you are allowed to when driving

spell v to say or write the letters forming a word in the right order

spice n a substance (often a powder)

made from plants used to give food a special flavor

spine *n* the bones at your back that keep your body straight

spoon *n* an object with a small, shallow bowl on a handle which is used for eating soup etc or cooking

sporting goods store *n* a shop selling sports equipment

sport *n* a physical activity that is done for enjoyment or to compete against others

sprain *v* to injure an ankle or another part of the body painfully without breaking it

stadium *n* an area where sports events are held

stairs *n.pl.* steps for moving from one level of a building to another

stamp *n* a small piece of paper stuck on items of mail to show that postage has been paid for; *v* to put a travel ticket into a machine to show it is being used for a particular journey

start *v* to begin an activity; to begin to function (such as a car engine)

starter *n* the first course of a meal

station *n* a place where you can get on or off passenger trains or buses

station wagon (U.S.) *n* a long car with space behind the seats for

loading

statue *n* a representation of a person or animal usually made of stone or metal

stay *v* to live somewhere for a short time; to wait; n time spent at a place

steal *v* to take something without permission

steep *adj* (of a hill etc) sloping at a high angle

sterling silver *n* a metal mixture containing a very large amount of the metal silver

sting *v* to feel or cause a sharp burning pain; *n* an injury caused by an insect

stomach *n* the part of the inside of the body where food is first broken down; the front part of the body between the chest and the waist

stomachache *n* a pain in the stomach

stop *v* to prevent; to cease movement or an action; *n* a point on a transport route where passengers can get on or off the vehicle

store directory *n* a listing or map of shops in a mall or shopping center

stove *n* a piece of kitchen equipment for cooking, roasting and baking

straight *adj* (of path etc) going in one direction without curves or turns; (of alcoholic drink) without anything added

strange *adj* not well known, unfamiliar, new; peculiar

stream *n* a narrow channel of naturally flowing water

stroller (U.S.) *n* a light, folding chair on wheels for a child

structure *n* an object made up of a number of parts which are held together in a certain way

student *n* a person who is at a school or university etc to learn

study *v* to take part in a course about a particular subject or subjects

stunning *adj* very impressive or attractive

subtitle *n* a printed translation of the dialog in a foreign film shown at the bottom of the screen in a cinema etc

subway *n* (U.S.) a rail network that (for the most part) runs under the ground; (U.K.) an underground passage or tunnel;

subway station *n* a place where you can get on or off underground trains

suit a set of smart or formal outer clothes meant to be worn together

suitcase *n* a container designed to hold or protect an object or objects used when traveling

sun *n* a star around which earth moves

and which gives off the light and warmth

sunblock *n* lotion or cream put on the skin to protect against sunburn

sunburn *n* reddening of the skin due to being in the sun for too long

sunglasses *n.pl.* darkened glasses for protecting the eyes from the sun

sunset *n* the time when the sun disappears below the horizon

sunstroke *n* fever and nausea due to too much sun in hot weather

super *adj* excellent; very good

supermarket *n* a large shop where food, drinks and other items are sold

supervise *v* to be in charge of an activity or a group of people

surfboard *n* a long narrow board which you stand on to move across water on waves

swallow *v* to take through the mouth and throat into the stomach

sweater *n* a warm piece of clothing for the upper body, often worn over a shirt

sweatshirt *n* a loose, long-sleeved sweater often worn for sport or relaxation

sweet *adj* having a taste like that of honey or sugar

sweets (U.K.) *n.pl.* sweet food made

with sugar and often containing chocolate, nuts, fruits etc

swell *v* to grow in size (usually after an injury)

swim *v* to move through water using your arms and legs to keep you above the surface

swimsuit *n* a piece of clothing worn for swimming or sunbathing

symbol *n* a mark, character or letter representing something

synagogue *n* a place where Jewish people go to pray

T

table *n* piece of furniture for placing objects on and eating meals from

tablet *n* a medicinal pill

take *v* to get hold of something; to remove something from a place

take away *v* to take something (such as food) with you

tampon *n* a small piece of material inserted into the vagina to absorb blood during menstruation

taste *n* to sense the flavor of something; to try something out

tax *n* a sum of money that has to be paid to the government or a local authority

taxi *n* a car in which people are transported to their destination of choice for an amount of money that depends on how far they travel

team *n* a group of sports players who play together against others; a collection of people working together

teaspoon *n* a small spoon used mainly for stirring and adding sugar to hot drinks

telephone *n* a piece of equipment with which you can talk to a person who is somewhere else

temple *n* a building or place where people come to pray

temporary *adj* for a limited period

tennis *n* a sport where two or four players hit a ball back and forth over a net using rackets

tent *n* a portable shelter made of canvas or other waterproof material

tent peg *n* a metal hook hammered into the ground to secure a tent

tent pole *n* a pole used to put up of a tent

terminal *n* an area or building at an airport where passengers get on and off airplanes

terracotta *n* a brownish-red substance used to make vases, bowls etc

terrible *adj* very bad, serious or unpleasant

text *n* an electronic message sent and received on a mobile phone; *v* to send an electronic message to someone

thank *v* to tell someone you are pleased or happy about something they said or did

thanks, thank you *int* a polite expression used when someone has said or done something kind

that *pron* used to identify a specific thing or person

theater (U.S.), theatre (U.K.) *n* a building where plays or productions are shown to an audience; (U.S.) a cinema

theft *n* the act of stealing

there *adv* in, at or to a place or position

thief *n* person who steals or has stolen something

thigh *n* the part of the leg between the knee and the hip

thirst *n* the need to drink liquid

this *pron* used to identify the person or thing that is present or near, or already mentioned

throat *n* the part of the body that runs from the back of the mouth down through the neck, down which food and drink are swallowed and air breathed

ticket *n* a card with which you are allowed to travel on a train, enter a public performance, a museum etc

ticket office *n* a place where tickets can be bought or picked up

tie *n* a strip of material worn and knotted around the neck of a shirt, usually by men

time *n* a specific hour of the clock; a period measured by seconds, minutes, hours, days, months and years

timetable *n* a printed list of the times of departure and arrival of trains or other modes of transport

tire (U.S.), tyre (U.K.) *n* a rubber covering of a wheel, often filled with air

tired *adj* to be in need of rest or sleep

tissues *n.pl.* disposable handkerchiefs

tobacconist *n* a shop that sells cigarettes and other goods for smokers

today *n* this present day; *adv* at the present time

toe *n* one of the five parts at the end of the foot that you can move

toenail *n* the hard part on the front of the toe

toilet *n* a bathroom or washroom

toilet-paper *n* paper for cleaning oneself after using the toilet

tomorrow *n* the day after tomorrow today

tongue *n* the soft part in the mouth used for tasting, swallowing and talking

tonight *n* the evening or night of today; this night

too *adv* as well; to a greater extent than desired, as in too big

tooth *n* one of the hard white objects in the mouth used for chewing or biting

toothpaste *n* a solution used together with a toothbrush to clean teeth

total *n* the whole or final amount of something

tough *adj* (of food) hard to chew

tour *n* a journey for pleasure which covers several locations

tourist *n* a person who is visiting somewhere for pleasure

tourist information office *n* a building or kiosk that provides information and services for visitors to a place

tow truck *n* a vehicle used to pick up and recover cars that are broken down or damaged

towel *n* a piece of material used for rubbing dry a person or thing

tower *n* a tall narrow structure (either part of a building or on its own)

town *n* a place where people live that is larger than a village but smaller than a city

town hall *n* a building with the offices of local officials or government

town square *n* an open public area in the middle of a town center

toy *n* an object which a child can play with

toy store *n* a shop that sells toys

track *n* the line of rails on which a train or vehicle runs; a course for races

traditional *adj* long-established or usual in a particular area or place

traffic light *n* a road signal lights to indicate that a vehicle must stop, slow down, or go

trail *n* a track for hiking

trail map *n* a map showing downhill ski routes

trailer *n* a vehicle, often for transporting goods, towed by another vehicle; (U.S.) a vehicle that can be towed by another vehicle and used as a vacation home or an office

train *n* a form of public transport that runs on rails

train station *n* the place where trains stop to allow passengers to get on or off

translate *v* to change words from one language into another and keep the same meaning

trash *n* things for thowing away

travel *v* to go from one place to another

travel agency *n* a business that sells vacations and travel tickets

travel sickness *n* (U.K.) nausea felt when traveling in a car, ship or aircraft

traveler's check (U.S.), traveller's cheque (U.K.) *n* a check that is securely paid for in advance and can used instead of cash when traveling

tree *n* a usually tall plant with a trunk, branches and leaves

trim *v* (of hair) to make neater by cutting a small amount off

trip *n* a short journey to a place

trolley *n* a large shopping basket on wheels

trousers *n.pl* a piece of clothing that covers the legs from the waist to the ankle

T-shirt *n* a shirt with short sleeves and no collar (usually made of cotton)

turn off *v* to make something (such as a light or TV) stop operating

turn on *v* to make something (such as a light or TV) start operating

TV *n* a device for sending sound and images on a screen

type *v* to write something on a computer, typewriter or smart phone using a keyboard

U

ugly *adj* not pleasing to look at; not attractive

umbrella *n* a portable device for keeping a person dry in the rain (usually a collapsable round piece of material on a long handle)

unattended *adj* not supervised or looked after

unconscious *adj* not awake or aware of surroundings

underground *n* (U.K.) a rail network that (for the most part) runs under the ground

underground station *n* a stop on an underground rail network

underpants *n* underwear worn by men or boys

understand *v* to follow the meaning of something

underwear *n* clothing worn under the main clothes (such as underpants or vest)

university *n* an institute of higher education and research

unleaded *adj* (of gasoline) without added lead (for the purposes of being more environmentally friendly)

upper *adj* situated on higher ground; located above something else; higher status

urgent *adj* requiring immediate

attention

use *v* to take something or put something into action for a specific purpose

username *n* a personal form of identification used when logging onto a site on the internet

utensil *n* a tool or object used in the home, as in cooking

V

vacancy *n* an available room in a hotel; an available position of employment

vacation *n* a time off work for relaxation; an overseas trip

vaccination *n* a treatment given to protect against disease and provide immunity

vacuum cleaner *n* an electrical appliance that sucks up dust and dirt

vagina *n* the passage between a female's outer sexual organs and the uterus

valid *adj* legally official or acceptable

valley *n* an area of lower land between hills or mountains

valuable *adj* worth a fairly large amount of money

value *n* the sum of money that something is worth

VAT *n* (U.K.) value-added tax, a sales

tax usually included the cost of goods bought

vegetarian *n* a person who does not eat meat and in some cases fish

viewpoint *n* a location with a very good view; a person's opinion

village *n* a place where people live that is smaller than a town

vineyard *n* a place where grapes are grown, usually to make wine

visit *v* to go to see a place or person; to travel somewhere or stay with someone for a short time

visiting hours *n* the time when people can come to a hospital to see a person

visually impaired *adj* not able to see normally

vitamin *n* any one of a number of natural substances essential for health (such as *vitamin C*), found in food or available in the form of tablets

volleyball *n* a sport played between two teams in which a ball is hit by hand over a net; the ball used to play the sport

vomit *v* to bring up the contents of your stomach through the mouth

W

wait v to stay in a place until a certain time or until a particular event occurs; n a delay

waiter n a man who brings food and drink to the guests in a restaurant

waiting room n a place where people can sit while waiting for a train, doctor etc

waitress n a woman who brings food and drink to the guests in a restaurant

wake v to make someone stop sleeping; to stop sleeping

wake-up call n an alarm call service in a hotel, usually available on request from reception

walk v to travel by foot; n a trip made on foot (often taken for pleasure); the route chosen for this

wallet n a pocket-sized folding case for carrying money and plastic cards

warm v to heat something up or to become hotter; adj at a (usually comfortable or pleasurable) high temperature

washing machine n a machine for the automatic washing of clothes

watch v to look at or observe something; n a small device with which you can see what time it is (usually worn on the wrist)

water skis n.pl. skis used for travelling over water when being pulled by a boat

waterfall n a part of a river where the water goes down from a high place

weather n the conditions in the atmosphere (such as sunshine or rain etc)

week n a period of seven days, esp. from Sunday to Saturday

weekend n the two-day period at the end of the working week, used by most peple for leisure (usually Saturday and Sunday in Europe and the U.S.A.)

weekly n occurring once every week

welcome v to greet someone with kindness or friendliness; you're welcome int used as a polite phrase in reply to someone who has just said thanks to you for something

west n the direction opposite to east; the point of the compass where the sun sets

what pron used in questions to ask for information specifying something; adj used before a noun in questions to ask which thing, kind, amount, number etc

wheelchair n a chair with wheels used to transport a person who cannot walk

wheelchair ramp n a sloping surface that provides access for wheelchair users to buildings or other facilities

when *adv*, *conj.* at what or which time

where *adv*, *conj.* at or in what place or situation,

white *adj* of the color of snow

who *pron* used in questions to ask which person or persons; used to refer back to a person or persons already mentioned in a sentence (as in the lady who spoke to me)

widow *n* a woman whose husband has died and who remains unmarried

wife *n* a married woman (in relation to her husband)

window *n* an opening in the wall or roof of a building, vehicle or other structure, usually fitted with glass

windsurfing board *n* a long narrow board with a mast and a sail on which a person can move across water

wine list *n* a menu of the wine selection in a restaurant

wireless internet *n* an internet connection service for which no cable is required (often abbreviated to Wi-Fi)

with *prep* accompanied by; possessing

withdraw *v* to take out of something (such as *to withdraw money from a bank*)

withdrawal *n* the act of taking money out of a bank account

without *prep* not having, lacking, free from

woman *n* an adult female

wool *n* the soft material made from a sheep's thick hair

work *v* to have as your job; (of a device) to function properly

wrap *v* to cover or enclose something

wrist *n* the joint connecting the hand and the arm

write *v* to form letters and words with a pen or other instrument

Y

year *n* the period of time taken for the earth to travel around the sun; a period of 12 months or 365 days (366 in leap years)

yellow *adj* of the color of lemons

yes *adv* used to give a positive answer to a question (opposite of no)

yesterday *n* the day immediately before today

young *adj* in the early stage of life, growth or development

youth hostel *n* a place providing cheap accommodation, usually for young people

Z

zoo *n* a place where living wild animals are kept and which is open to the public

Berlitz®

speaking your language

phrase book & dictionary
phrase book & CD

Available in: Arabic, Cantonese Chinese, Croatian, Czech, Danish, Dutch, English, Finnish*, French, German, Greek, Hebrew*, Hindi, Hungarian*, Indonesian, Italian, Japanese, Korean, Latin American Spanish, Mandarin Chinese, Mexican Spanish, Norwegian, Polish, Portuguese, Romanian*, Russian, Spanish, Swedish, Thai, Turkish, Vietnamese

*Book only